# HUMANITIES IN PRIMARY EDUCATION
## History, Geography and Religious Education in the Classroom

**Don Kimber, Nick Clough, Martin Forrest,
Penelope Harnett, Ian Menter and
Elizabeth Newman**

**David Fulton Publishers**
London

David Fulton Publishers Ltd
2 Barbon Close, London WC1N 3JX

First published in Great Britain by David Fulton Publishers 1995

Note: The right of Don Kimber, Nick Clough, Martin Forrest, Penelope Harnett, Ian Menter and Elizabeth Newman to be identified as the authors of this work has been asserted by them in accordance with the Copyright, Designs and Patents Act 1988.

Copyright © Don Kimber, Nick Clough, Martin Forrest, Penelope Harnett, Ian Menter and Elizabeth Newman

*British Library Cataloguing in Publication Data*

A catalogue record for this book is available from the British Library

ISBN 1-85346-342-6

Typeset by The Harrington Consultancy
Printed in Great Britain by BPC Books and Journals Ltd., Exeter

# Contents

# Humanities Education

Humanities education is concerned with human beliefs, experience and behaviour, and the expression of these.

It is about the past – as things were; the present – as things are; the future – what things are likely to be and what they might/ought to be.

It is about individual experience, about groups and nations and the whole human experience. It is concerned with the immediate and local, and with the distant and global.

It is concerned with the relationships between people, between people and the environment and the relationship of people to their spiritual worlds.

Humanities education is concerned with understanding, knowledge, skills and values. Schools should help young people to understand, know, do and value in the realm of the humanities.

Rex Beddis (1931–88)

# Introduction

This book has emerged out of the collective experience of six colleagues who work together at the Faculty of Education of the University of the West of England, in Bristol.

It is a project that has been in our minds for some time, particularly in the mind of one of us, Don Kimber, who has provided the driving force to bring the writing to fruition. Writing collaboratively is always an interesting process and we have had many discussions about it. We considered naming 'first drafters' of each chapter as its author/s. However, the process has been so strongly characterised by discussion, debate and revision that we decided that this would be inappropriate. It has been our intention that the whole book should have consistency in substance and in style. Chapters draw on the experience of all members of the team. Although each chapter was initially drafted by one or two individuals, these drafts were then read and discussed by the rest of the team. We not only commented and rewrote, we were also able to feed in exemplary material from a variety of sources, which we have tended to refer to as 'case study material'.

The use of such material is a feature of the books in the series to which this volume contributes. But it is also consistent with the view of learning and teaching which underpins this volume (and indeed the series). The twin strands here are a social constructivist model of learning and a reflective teaching model of pedagogy. Through reflecting on our experiences and evaluating our intentions, practices and outcomes, not only do we learn, but we also enrich the learning of those children, pupils and students with whom we are working.

In Chapter 1 we set the scene by visiting a small primary school in Gloucestershire. Drawing on this account we then set out to define the scope of humanities in the primary school and to elaborate our underlying model of teaching and learning in more detail.

In Chapters 2, 3, and 4 we focus our attention on history, geography and religious education respectively and consider the contribution which these subjects can make to our own and children's understandings of the society in which we live. We will draw attention also to ways in which cross-curricular opportunities readily present themselves even when we might have one particular subject area in mind.

Those chapters comprising the middle section – Chapters 5, 6, and 7 – deal with cross-curricular approaches in relation to some key contemporary themes in the teaching and learning of humanities, namely environmental education, citizenship education and education for life in a new and developing Europe.

The final set of Chapters – 8, 9, and 10 – provide an opportunity to look more closely at some of the broader pedagogical questions which arise in the field of humanities, and provide an opportunity to synthesise some of the points raised in previous discussion. In Chapter 8 we focus on the learning of humanities through 'staged events'. The discussion draws together ideas about active and experiential learning. The role of the teacher, questions of pupil assessment and the organisation of teaching are the topics of Chapter 9. The discussion in Chapter 10 draws threads together and also reminds the reader of the wider social and cultural context within which primary humanities is taught and learned.

It is with pleasure that we gratefully acknowledge the support of the numerous teachers and children in schools who have contributed to our understanding of primary humanities. We have also been assisted greatly by teachers and students working on in-service and pre-service courses at our Faculty.

Amongst those whose work has been drawn upon we would like to thank the staff and pupils of the following schools, most of which are in Bristol: St Anne's CE Primary, Oldland Common; Romney Avenue Juniors; Sefton Park Juniors; Cabot Primary; St Barnabas CE Primary; Callicroft Infants; Doncaster Road Juniors; Eastcombe School; Hambrook Primary; The Park Primary; St Peter and St Paul RC Primary; Holy Family RC Primary; St Helen's CE Primary, Alveston; Pilning Primary; Downs Park Day Nursery School; St Stephen's CE Juniors, Soundwell. The work of the following individuals has also been drawn upon: Paul and Sarah Jackson (formerly of St Werburgh's City Farm); Sarah Foxton; Marion Loveridge; Joyce Richards; Bob Callicott; Estelle Loft; Emma Smith; Cath Monks; Sally Mlewa; Wendy Stillwell; Chris Howard; Paula Knee; Jeff Hague; June Saunders; Sue Pritchard; Veronica Lee and colleagues; Tina Hickman; Heidi Chiswell; Emma Dangerfield; Lisa Tribe; Cathy Hall; Pippa Davies; and Sharonjit Bassir.

In writing the case study material, where it is appropriate to do so, we have given the real names of schools and teachers although not of children. In other instances, we have made the participants and locations anonymous, either because we have insufficient detail or because we did not have express permission to give names.

Many colleagues have supported us in various ways. In particular we wish to thank: colleagues in our Faculty's audio-visual aids department, Richard Egan, Paul Gilbert and Tim Knowles; Lyn Cooke and Heather Watts for administrative and secretarial assistance; Jane Tarr and Bereket Yebio for their contributions (particularly to the discussion within Chapter 6); Andrew Pollard for his encouragement and Mary Jane Drummond for her very helpful critical reading and advice.

We also thank Philip Wiegand and Falmer Press for permission to publish two maps from *Places in the Primary School* (1992). Last but not least, we thank Helen Tann for allowing us to use her photograph of children at work together on the front cover.

### The Primary Curriculum Series

This innovative series is an ideal means of supporting professional practice in the post-Dearing era, when a new focus on the quality of teaching and learning is possible. The series promotes reflective teaching and active forms of pupil learning. The books explore the implications of these commitments for curriculum and curriculum-related issues.

The argument of each book flows in, around and among a variety of case studies of classroom practice, introducing them, probing, analysing and teasing out their implications before moving on to the next stage of the argument. The case study material varies in source and form – children's work, teachers' work, diary entries, drawings, poetry, literature, interviews. The vitality and richness of primary school practice are conveyed, together with the teacher expertise on which these qualities are based.

### Series Editors

Mary Jane Drummond is Tutor in Education, University of Cambridge, Institute of Education, and Andrew Pollard is Professor in the Faculty of Education, University of the West of England, Bristol.

### Series Titles

# CHAPTER ONE

# Exploring Humanities in the Primary Curriculum

## 'What is special about being human?'

This is a key question which will inform our thinking about primary children and their learning in humanities in primary classrooms. What would we seek to help children learn about themselves? How do they give meaning to their world and other people in it? What are some of the human values which we as adults and teachers would try to help them to clarify for themselves as they grow, as we hope they will, to take a responsible role in their community?

There are other central questions which we will explore. What is the nature of humanities education, and how can this relate to learning in the primary classroom? How do we see humanities relating to the overall (National) curriculum? How do children give meaning to the world around them, especially as it relates to humanities?

How do children best learn humanities? This is another key question. We might be involved with children formally in the school or classroom. There will be many other times when we are casually interacting with them in a non-school context. This could be in the supermarket, at a bus stop, or over the garden wall, if not at home. Frequently, often without our recognising it, we are trying to impart selected human values, knowledge, and understandings to children (no doubt reflecting our own preferences, not to say prejudices). Are there particular ways in which we should go about helping children learn 'humanities', based on well-defined, specific, recognised processes and conditions which more effectively help them to learn in general?

To provide a starting-point for exploring these central questions – 'What is the nature of primary humanities?' and 'How do children best

2

learn humanities?' – we can reflect on the following scene in a small Gloucestershire school. It can illustrate how easily various aspects of humanities and of children's learning can arise.

## 'The person that did something'

It is a warm and sunny June morning in the Cotswolds. The village of Eastcombe is perched on a hill above the Stroud valley. Along the lane on the way to school, birds are singing, and fresh flowers are plentiful in the grassy verges. The peaceful scene accords with the typical picturesque postcard images we hold of such rural retreats.

The sound of children singing comes from the compact, stone-built village school. Inside 70 children from ages 5 to 11 are accompanied on the piano as they sing 'When I needed a neighbour, were you there, were you there?'.

All the children are clustered in what is now one classroom. Originally this was the major part of a large school hall. Some of the area has been partitioned off to provide some space for an adjoining classroom.

Mrs Veronica Lee, the headteacher, and her three colleagues, are leading school assembly. The children settle and listen attentively after their rendition of 'When I needed a neighbour', which they had seemingly enjoyed.

'At great expense', begins Mrs Lee, 'for your enjoyment' – children are smiling, already aware that her words are not necessarily to be taken too literally – 'we have been working hard on preparing a theatrical event for you. It has been very carefully rehearsed since we wrote it yesterday dinner time'.

Another colleague, bedecked in stunning floral headgear, stands up, and launches into telling a story of a traveller on a train to York. Mrs Lee and the two other teachers are sitting in a line of three chairs behind her. While remaining mainly seated, they occasionally stand up, and join in acting out some of the characters, or scenes as appropriate:

'A man is travelling on the train to York. Unfortunately he finds himself mixed up with a bunch of football hooligans on the train.'

The seated trio produce football scarves, wave them in the air, and break into some familiar chants from the terraces. The teachers are enjoying this as much as the children.

'... the traveller gets mugged by the hooligans. They rob him, take all his money, and leave him unconscious ...'.

The storyteller goes on to describe how a vicar on the train comes along, is not sure how best to react to this situation, but stops to offer a prayer for the man. 'A-a-a-men' is piously intoned by the seated trio. Children chuckle.

Then the social worker with experience of working with children from an inner city council comes along. 'I just le-erve children' she oozes. But she feels unable to cope with the traveller who has been mugged. 'Let me get a drink at the bar' is the cry of this member of the trio. She walks unsteadily across 'the stage', murmuring 'I just le-erve children'. Children again appreciate this.

A third traveller on the train was a 'mean, no-good punk rock group leader'. He sees the plight of the man and acts. He stops the train, gives the man £20 for a new coat, and calls an ambulance to take him to hospital. The traveller is now safe and well looked after.

Mrs Lee rose to her feet. She looked around the room to get the attention of all the children. 'When it came to the crunch,' she asked, 'who was the next door neighbour to the traveller?'

A 9-year-old girl says 'The man that did something for him'.

Mrs Lee: Yes, the person that did something for him. Who is my neighbour?

Girl: Everybody.

Mrs Lee: I will now tell a similar story. But listen carefully.

Mrs Lee then told a more conventional version of the bible story of the Good Samaritan, with the familiar elements. On the road from Jerusalem to Jericho, a travelling Jew is attacked by thieves who leave him for dead. A priest comes by but hurries on. Then comes the Levite, a Temple assistant, who similarly passes by on the other side of the road. The Samaritan, a member of an ethnic minority group despised by the Jews, then arrives. He stops, gives the victim water, bathes his wounds, and takes him to a village to rest for a few days to recover. He leaves money to cover any expenses.

Mrs Lee: Jesus asked 'Who was his neighbour?'

Child: The man who helped him.

Mrs Lee: How were these two stories related? Did they differ? John?

John: This was a modern-day version of it.

The children were then divided into two groups, and they joined in singing another song ('Seek ye first the Kingdom of God') as a round.

By their general responses, the children enjoyed hearing this story of The Good Samaritan and all appeared to listen attentively to both versions of it. At the time, they also had a clear idea of what it implied in terms of being a 'good neighbour'. This was also evident in discussions with small groups of 8- and 9-year-old children in the session after the 'assembly'. They appreciated that the stories were to help them understand how people should behave one to another. Sensitive and caring relationships were built on notions of 'helping those in need', and often the rationale was simply along the lines of 'How would you like to be treated if you were in their position?' (9-year-old girl). Such considerations of how people relate successfully to others is essential in the learning of humanities. The children also realised that this concept was pertinent to them, not simply how others should act. It was for them to try to practise in their own relationships.

In continuing this initial exploration of the nature of humanities, further clues as to how children appreciate the nature of humanities (as adults might perceive humanities) are offered in these snatches of dialogue. They were recorded in a subsequent visit to the school, when, after watching a video of the Good Samaritan assembly, we were able to discuss aspects of the story with 8-year-old children in small groups.

The following quotations are short extracts taken in sequence from a 20-minute discussion with one group of the 8- and 9-year olds.

*Teacher:* If we look at the time line up there on the wall, whereabouts was it when Jesus lived. Can you see? It says...
2 or 3 children offer ideas.
*Teacher:* Yes, you are nearly right. Right at the end there can you see where it says 43 and then 0. One thousand, nine hundred and ninety three years ago Jesus was born. Jesus lived in a land called...
*Leonie:* Jerusalem.
*Teacher:* You are very nearly right. Land of Palestine. Can you see? Have you got a map? This is the sea. You said Jerusalem. If we look there, that place is...can your read it?
*Leonie:* Jericho.
*Teacher:* Have you heard of the name?
*Leonie:* In the story.
*Barry:* North [looking at the map and pointing].
*Teacher:* Quite right – that's North.
*Eileen:* The traveller – he got robbed.
*Vincent:* And punched and kicked.
*Alison:* They took his coat and money.

The children were talking about the experiences of the traveller mugged on the road from Jerusalem. Helped by the prompting of the teacher–interviewer, they were able to apply the story to the history timeline which was displayed prominently upon the classroom wall. They also very readily applied some of the map-reading skills which they had. Indeed Barry volunteered his understanding of the map symbol for 'North', for the benefit of the rest of us. This in turn helped to sustain the interest and involvement of other children, recognising that their contributions would likely be accepted and credited. The conversation then returns to the plight of the Jew travelling to Jericho.

A minute or two later it can be seen how discussion naturally enabled children to express ideas of place and of landscapes.

*Teacher:* But it was very rough wild countryside. In fact,...
*Brian:* [interrupting or contributing before a formal invitation to speak] They did not have many signs and things.
*Teacher:* There weren't any signs. Now can you see what sort of country that looks like in the picture. Can you see, Rachel?
*Rachel:* Is it all sand?
*Teacher:* It is all sand.
*Rachel:* It looks like all hills, and it's bumpy, and sand on.
*Teacher:* Bumpy and sand. What do we call places which are very hot – very hot and very sandy, and little rain?
*Brian:* Erhm...
*Teacher:* Beginning with 'D'. Do you know Benjamin?
*Benjamin:* Desert.
*Teacher:* Desert. Desert – good. Have you all heard of deserts?
*Rachel and others:* Yes.
*Teacher:* Part of Palestine was like this, other parts had large cities.

In a later part of the discussion the children are offering their ideas about the work of a priest, and weighing up the rights and wrongs of what should have been the appropriate response of those who came across the traveller who had been mugged and left for dead.

*Teacher:* The first person who came along was a ...p – pr -
*Brian:* Priest.
*Teacher:* Yes – What does a priest do? What's a priest's job? Do you know, Tina?
*Tina:* To help people.
*Teacher:* Yes, they should help people, but then perhaps we should all help people.
*Brian:* I know.
*Teacher:* Tammy, what else does a priest do. Anything else?
*Tammy:* They go to church.
*Teacher:* They go to church, yes, anything else?
*Mark:* I – they tell people things in church.
*Teacher:* Yes, they tell people things in church, so a priest would

have been in the Temple, or the Jewish synagogue and helping people know what to do to be right. The priest hurried on his way didn't he?
*Child:* Yeh.
*Teacher:* ...and left the man there.
*Anthony:* Really, if he was – erm – was not on his way to church he would have stopped going and helped him.

These brief extracts from a 20-minute discussion with a group of 8- and 9-year old children offer a flavour of some of the various facets of humanities which can be involved in a discussion of a simple story with which children can identify. Let us now review in a little more systematic way the nature of humanities.

## What is the nature of primary humanities?

This account of an assembly and a discussion in a Gloucestershire primary school indicates very well some of the key features of primary humanities. Firstly, we get the sense that humanities are very much part of the culture of a school as well as of timetabled subjects. Secondly, we get a sense of how different 'subjects' within the humanities overlap significantly. Thirdly, we see how cross-curricular elements are served by the humanities. There is a fourth aspect of this which has particular significance in the primary school, that the humanities very often complement a topic-based approach to the curriculum.

Before we proceed any further we do however need to attempt to define what we mean by humanities. Blyth (1990), in his book on assessing learning in humanities, suggests three perspectives constituting the humanities, namely historical, geographical and social-science perspectives. At the level of higher education, the humanities have traditionally been viewed as also involving the fields or areas of English and literature.

An alternative way of approaching humanities is not to list the subjects to be included but to capture its distinctive contribution to thought and knowledge. This is no easy matter, of course, but it is important, if we are to justify the inclusion of the humanities within the primary curriculum. We wish to argue and to demonstrate in this book that the distinctive feature of the humanities as an area of learning is that they enable young children to develop an understanding of their own place and identity within the world in which they are growing up: indeed that they learn what is special about being human. It is not that other areas of learning do nothing of this, rather that this is the central and distinctive contribution of the humanities.

But such an approach takes us immediately into another dimension, that of values. If we are saying that this subject is about personal and social identity, then questions of values, norms, and of morality, are right at the centre of our discussion. The recent clamour for children to be taught the difference between 'right' and 'wrong' has, in a sense, reminded us that the humanities have an important contribution to make in this domain. To put it bluntly, the humanities have a strong political and moral dimension.

If we were to pursue such a stipulative definition in a pure sense, and were to return to the question of subjects, we would no doubt wish to claim social science and a whole range of cultural and literary studies within the area. But our definition needs to have a pragmatic aspect too, so that the reader might connect with children in classrooms. The National Curriculum, as presently defined, stipulates that English is one of the core subjects and has a clear and separate existence. Thus, for the purpose of this book, we do not include English within our definition. Secondly, social science is not recognised as a subject at all within the National Curriculum, therefore we do not deal with this as such. Nevertheless we will repeatedly see how social science perspectives do contribute in the humanities whether to 'subjects' (e.g. history and geography) or to cross-curricular themes, (e.g. citizenship). The third feature of our definition of humanities is to include the compulsory (yet non-National Curriculum) subject of religious education. As our introductory account indicated, religious and moral elements in the school curriculum can provide a very rich vein for developing children's understanding of themselves as individuals and as social beings.

Our definition therefore incorporates the three subjects: history, geography and religious education. Part of the purpose of the book is to look at the relationship between these subjects in the primary curriculum. However, we are also interested in how the humanities relate to other subjects and indeed how various cross-curricular approaches can not only enhance the humanities curriculum in itself, but can lead on to make a rich contribution to the primary curriculum as a whole. In particular we explore National Curriculum cross-curricular themes of environmental education and education for citizenship.

To summarise and support the discussion so far we will make a brief return to Eastcombe to show how these subjects and themes are exemplified in that account.

The story of the Good Samaritan was used to prompt knowledge and ideas about:

- *History* – chronology, the sequence of events in the story, the setting of events in the story in the Near East nearly 2,000 years ago; the importance of historical influences upon how people act in a current situation (Samaritans were longstanding enemies of Jews who despised them as members of a minority ethnic group).

- *Geography* – characteristics of people, place and environment; rural and urban landscapes; using maps.
- *Religious education* – who is my neighbour and (why) should it concern me? The role of a priest. Expectations of moral behaviour.
- *Environmental education* – some of the phenomena around us which can fashion and give identity to environments; how can we improve environments to make them more friendly and less threatening?
- *Citizenship* – the Levite who more or less said 'But I was only following the rules, Guv'; in which sorts of situation should we break the rules? Personal and social responsibility.

Having reviewed the nature of humanities, we conclude this chapter by attempting to answer a third key question – how do children learn humanities? This will enable us to discuss teaching approaches too.


## How do children learn humanities?

Underpinning our discussion in the following chapters will be a view about the nature of learning and how it is best supported and fostered. We see learning as an active and continuous process whereby learners adjust and modify their existing understandings as they encounter fresh experiences and information. This occurs not just in school but in many different social situations.

We recognise that learning is not a solitary process, but rather a dynamic activity where social interaction is important in developing children's understandings. Social and cognitive skills as well as knowledge are acquired through this interaction. But this is not all; values and culture are also transmitted. This background of culture and social history provides a powerful influence on learning; it provides the lenses through which children interpret their experiences and make them meaningful for themselves.

When Mrs Lee and her colleagues were preparing the morning assembly, some account was taken of the children's culture. The characters introduced in the modern version of the Good Samaritan were recognised by the children. They were able to identify the good neighbour in the mean-no-good-punk-rock-leader and this contemporary account helped children interpret the more traditional bible story.

Throughout the book, we have sought to include children's

interpretations and responses to learning situations. This has provided a means for assessing children's current understandings and values, emanating not only from their work in the classroom but also from their other experiences outside the confines of the school.

Many of the ideas developed and much of the knowledge which was transmitted during the morning would have been familiar to the children. The skill of Mrs Lee and her colleagues lay in providing opportunities for children to synthesise, and then to develop further, existing understandings. Through discussion with their peers and support from Mrs Lee, children were able to move forward in their learning. This model of the learning process finds support from Vygotsky who described learning occurring as learners cross their zone of proximal development (ZPD). This zone is defined as:

> the distance between the actual developmental level (of the child) as
> determined through problem solving and the level of potential development
> as determined through problem solving under adult guidance or in
> collaboration with more capable peers. (Vygotsky, 1978:86)

To move forward in their understanding, learners need help across this ZPD. Help can be provided by a more knowledgeable other, who recognises the stage which learners have reached and can assist them to move beyond their existing ZPD and acquire fresh understandings. To do this successfully, the knowledgeable other requires information about the learner's current perceptions as well as particular knowledge which will help the learner to move on further across the ZPD.

This model of the teaching and learning process is made explicit in Figure 1.1. The assistance offered by the reflective agent in this model is based on the agent's perception of children's particular needs and of the stage which they have reached in their work. Children are moved forward in their learning by the support and instruction offered by the reflective agent. The reflective agent may be the teacher, but could be any other more knowledgeable persons, including the peer group. During the morning's activities which centred on the Good Samaritan, many examples were recorded where the teacher intervened to help children. There were also instances where it was apparent that through discussion, the children were helped to clarify their ideas and to draw on each other for different views on the meaning and purpose of the story.

We reiterate here the emphasis on the social nature of learning – that learning is not a solitary activity, but one where learners are moved on in their understanding by interaction with other people. The provision, therefore, of opportunities for interaction where children can acquire new concepts and ideas and challenge their existing ones is important.

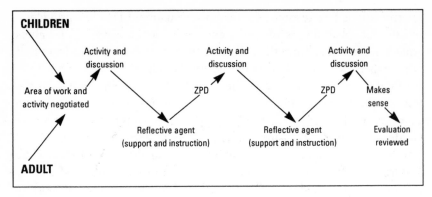

**Figure 1.1** A social constructive model of roles in the teaching–learning process (Source: Pollard and Tann, 1994: 112.)

Language, and in particular talk, underpins this view of learning. The three interlinking aspects of talk shown in Figure 1.2 can all contribute towards the collaborative learning processes which will be explored in the book. Following the drama of the Good Samaritan in the hall, all three aspects of talk could be seen to be developing as children worked in the classroom. Social interaction was encouraged as groups of children commented on the morning's activities; they listened to each other and responded to each other's comments, often repeating what others had said.

> *Teacher:* The road was not like the one outside the school because...
> *Benjamin:* ...because they did not have diggers and buses and things.
> *Andrew:* Diggers and things.

Through talk children are able to clarify their ideas and express them to others in the learning situation.

> *Andrew:* Really if he was erm was not on his way to church he would have stopped going and helped him.
> *Teacher:* Yeh, the priest was in a hurry.
> *Matthew:* He didn't want to get involved, or he would be late for the service, and also all the people...all the people stay at home.
> *Teacher:* Matthew was right there because the priest was anxious that he might be late.
> *Benjamin:* It doesn't really matter if he was late.
> *Matthew:* It would.
> *Teacher:* Benjamin why do you think it wouldn't matter if he was late?
> *Benjamin:* If he had stopped and helped him he would, erm, he

would be, em, have helped God, and be kind and loving. If he had not...if he did not go...back to the church, he would not have been there to tell people stories and things.

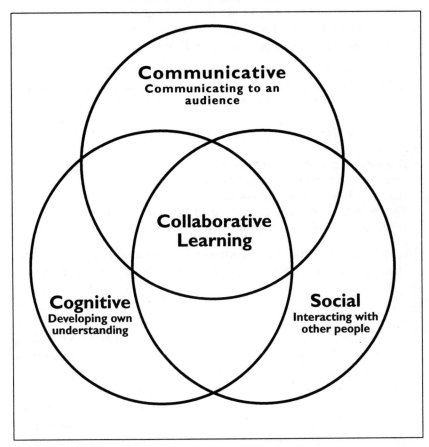

**Figure 1.2** Forms of talk in collaborative learning (Adapted from Norman, 1990.)

In this conversation, the children were able to articulate their different points of views about the event. Matthew built on Andrew's original comments in the first two lines. Benjamin however, interpreted the episode in a different light; he adds a fresh perspective as to whether the priest should have been criticised for leaving the Samaritan. Benjamin is using speech to clarify his thoughts on the episode; as he talks the 'erms' suggest that he is thinking through alternatives to the story. He is talking also to convince the others of his point of view and consequently thinking carefully through his reasons. The discussion here has enabled the children to share their thoughts, which has enriched and extended their original viewpoints and enabled them to recognise alternative versions. The communicative, cognitive and social aspects of talk are thus all interlinked within this discussion.

Talking is a valuable way of acquiring fresh information. The teacher was able to build on what children already knew about the roads to elaborate further on the state of roads in Palestine.

*Teacher:* What sort of road do you think it was like?

*Matthew:* No, it was like, sort of like ... sand, and mud and twigs.

*Teacher:* The road was not like the one outside the school because...

*Benjamin:* Because they did not have diggers and buses and things.

*Andrew:* Diggers and things.

*Teacher:* Did not have what we call...

*Andrew:* [interrupting] Pavement.

*Teacher:* Yes, like a pavement, and tar. But they did have other roads which were sometimes made of stones.

The importance of making opportunities for such talk in the classroom will be a recurrent theme running through the book. Such opportunities for enabling talk will frequently be intertwined with the involvement of children in 'active learning'. Moving away from an overdependence on a mode of teaching where the teacher imparts knowledge (the facts) to children who are the passive receivers, the case studies and learning experiences will often show children actively involved in the process. Collaboration with others, enquiry based learning, problem solving, children drawing upon their own resources and knowledge – these are some of the sorts of experiences used to help children learn humanities. We will also see how these can be successful not only in motivating children, but also in helping children of all abilities achieve success in the classroom.

# CHAPTER TWO

# *Roots and Traditions*

This chapter will begin by looking at people's curiosity about their past and the past around them. History will be defined as a critical study of the past and discussion will focus on what part of the past should be taught. We give consideration to different opinions, including those of children. Reference will be made to the National Curriculum and the views of historical knowledge and ways of working in history embodied within the National Curriculum document.

The view that history is essentially about people we explore through three case studies. Different source materials were used in these studies and their value as evidence of the past will be discussed. Children's abilities to use source materials and the different interpretations which can arise will be described. We conclude the chapter by discussing how we can extend children's interest and understanding of history.

## Children and adults in relation to time

*Who am I?*

'Tell me about when I was little.' 'Tell me about what I did when I was a baby'. These are frequent requests from young children. Children appear to have an insatiable curiosity to hear about themselves and the things which they did when they were younger. Perhaps children's interest in their personal history stems from noting the momentous changes which have occurred to them during their young life. The facts that they could once squeeze into a tiny Baby-gro, hold a bottle or drinking cup or could only shuffle about on their bottoms hold endless fascination for young children. By learning about their past, children can begin to establish more of their identity; placing themselves in time can help them recognise the uniqueness of their own experience and their own personal history. As well as helping to inform the present a study of their past can also help children look to the future, to that time 'when I'm grown up'; part of children's predictions and speculations will have roots in their past, in what they have already changed from. In this respect the past forms a reference point for children in helping them to establish their present identity as part of a process of what they will become.

Interest in the past is not confined to one's own life however. In Jane Austen's *Persuasion*, we meet the character:

> ...Sir Walter Elliot, of Kellynch-hall, in Somersetshire, a man, who for his own amusement, never took up any book but the Baronetage; there he found occupation for an idle hour, and consolation in a distressed one. (Austen, 1965:3)

Tracing one's pedigree remains no longer the privilege or interest of the rich or titled and many people are concerned to dig out their roots and discover their family genealogies as some of the full reading rooms of local record offices can testify. Yet to understand our families' histories more fully we need a background against which we can place these births, marriages and deaths. Family decisions and events need to be set within the appropriate time context; this background is necessary to explain the lives of our ancestors.

The historical context provides opportunities for understanding one's own place and one's family's place in the past. The wartime slogan, 'What did you do in the war, Daddy?', struck a note which propagandists recognised would be effective. Children and families seek a context in which to place their history. In more recent times, people have talked about what they were doing when news of Kennedy's assassination was broadcast. (Colleagues have different recollections: one recalls watching her mother ironing; another remembers sitting next to his future wife whilst her mother broke the news.) More recently, people have discussed how they heard news of Mandela's release from prison. There is a fascination in snatching a moment in time, when world events are being shaped and yet ordinary lives are continuing in much the same routine way.

So we have a personal interest in our own history and in the relationship of our experience with the outside world. We like to see our place or our family's place in the world which has passed.

## The past around us

We learn our personal histories often through word of mouth, through the memories of those close to us who have watched us grow up or who have heard the family stories from older relations. Oral tradition is important. But we are surrounded by mementoes of our past too; not only of our own past but of a much wider heritage. Our streets, our towns and cities, our villages and the countryside all bear the imprints of former times. Interest in these remains and in what has been called our 'heritage' seems to be continually increasing. We can learn about different groups in society whether rich or poor, young or old, living in the recent past as well as more distant times, through visits to stately homes, heritage sites and museums. Costume dramas and documentaries on TV, magazines and books all provide more information. Re-enactments of civil war battles, medieval feasts or Victorian school days also provide opportunities to participate in the past.

The past is very marketable too. The heritage tradition can be continued in our own homes and certain interior designers have sought to perpetuate the myth of the farmhouse kitchen or the country cottage look. The enormous sales of artefacts from heritage and museum shops all indicate popular enthusiasm for the past and the desire to recreate part of a bygone age.

Yet the heritage tradition can promote an unrealistic and often romantic interpretation of the past. It can encourage us to view the past as a golden age, set apart from the pressures and problems current in contemporary society. Adults can often look back on their childhood memories to summers where it never rained, when fireworks were enormous, when holidays went on for ever and schooldays were the happiest of days. The passage of time dims recollections of what life was actually like.

Romantic memories of the past, however, often belie what really occurred. The rural idyll would not be recognised by hardworking farm labourers trying to bring up their families on a subsistence wage. Which Victorian traditions and values would we seek to preserve from that age of child labour and prostitution, terrible poverty and disease? On closer inspection, the cosy interpretation of the past fostered by some politicians and image makers does not always relate to evidence derived from the time.

The past is all around us; it has helped to shape our lives, but we need to examine it critically. The examples above demonstrate the importance of encouraging children to question the generalisations and stereotypes which can easily be assumed. Indeed historians claim that we all know about the past; it is only when we critically engage with the material that we are really studying history:

> The past embraces everything that ever happened and history embraces, chronicles, investigates and explains the past. (DES, 1990: para 1.2)

We turn now to discuss the selection of history to be taught in school. We look first at the choices which children might make before examining some of the controversies arising from the selection of National Curriculum history.

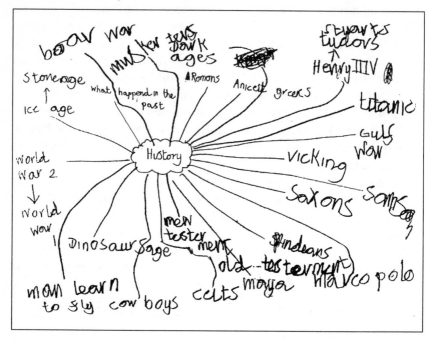

**Figure 2.1** History Brainstorming (boys)

## Which part of the past?

*Children's views*

By the time children reach the age of nine they already have very decided views on what constitutes history. This in part must be governed by what children are taught in school but also we must take into account their own particular perspective and interests outside school. West (1986) has argued that children's knowledge about the past is more considerable than is generally recognised by adults and suggests that at least two-thirds of this knowledge is acquired from sources outside the school setting.

An interesting exercise is to ask children to brainstorm their ideas about history. In the brainstorm represented by Figure 2.1 a group of 9- and 10-year-old boys summarise history as things which happened in the past and then select particular events and periods of time. They recognise periods of history, linked with what they have already studied at school, for example the Vikings, the Maya, the Greeks. Famous people are noted too, such as Marco Polo. But included in their list are items which they themselves have found personally interesting such as the Three Musketeers, the world wars and the Titanic.

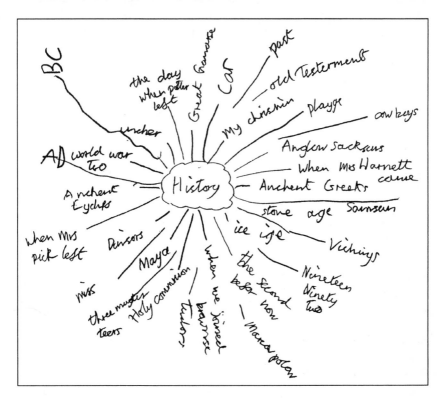

**Figure 2.2** History brainstorming (girls)

Contrast this with the brainstorm from a group of girls of the same age (Figure 2.2); again periods and famous people appear. The contrast arises from the girls' recognition that they themselves are part of history. They include personal events, recognising the importance of these things for their own lives. And surely history must include some recognition that we are all part of history and that we are making history today.

*Landmarks of British history?*

Mrs Thatcher asserted, 'Children should know the great landmarks of British history' (Kearney, 1994). Controversy however surrounds the definition of what these landmarks should be. Beneath the headline in the *Daily Mirror*, 'Out goes 1066 and all that', Richard Garner (1994) noted major omissions in the Dearing Committee's proposals for the revision of the history National Curriculum (SCAA, 1994a). These included the names of kings and queens, famous people such as Nelson, Wellington, Florence Nightingale and Clive of India and the battles at Agincourt, Waterloo and Trafalgar. Other commentators in the press were dismayed to find Guy Fawkes and the Plague and Fire of London missing. Feelings run high on preserving our landmarks; 'Britain's glorious past banished from lessons', screamed *The Sun* (5.5.94) and readers were invited to phone 'You the Jury' to express their views on whether 'our children be taught about Britain's heritage, or should Nelson and Waterloo be taken off the curriculum?' (Roycroft-Davis, 1994).

The debate focuses on what counts as British heritage; the facts to be taught will inevitably be influenced by the story we want to tell. In a famous analogy E.H. Carr (1964) suggested that the historian's work in selecting facts is like a fisherman catching fish in the ocean. Facts do not lie neatly on the 'fishmonger's slab', but have to be caught. The type of facts caught will depend on where the historian chooses to fish and the tackle which is used. As we make our selection of historical facts we will take into account aspects of our past which we deem important – yet this can vary according to our current perceptions. If we believe we are members of an homogeneous society with shared communal values, we look to the past to explain how these shared values have come about in our democratic institutions, our economic decision making and through the cultural heritage and social mechanisms of our society. On the other hand we might celebrate the diversity of our society, and this time our search through the past will include different incidents and features of past lives which mark and maintain our differences. This possibility has always been true; for example many western nineteenth century historians looked on the past as part of man's inexorable march towards the creation of a civilised society. The aspects of the past which they chose to study emphasised how this march and consequent progress came about. Historians can select their facts to match their perspective; perhaps this is why General Secretary Kruschev of the USSR was led to claim that: 'Historians are dangerous people. They are capable of upsetting everything' (quoted by HMI, 1985:1).

During the Dearing Review of the National Curriculum in 1994, the then Secretary of State for Education, John Patten, expressed strong views on the story he wanted children to hear:

> We must not allow our children to be robbed of their birthright of knowledge about our country's history. To have national pride should be seen as a virtue, not a vice. We in this country have a history built up over long ages, from Roman times and even before. (reported by Shrimsley, 1994)

It is interesting to note here how Patten tried to emphasise Britain's unique identity. This country does indeed have a history going back beyond Roman times, but this is not unique – so does every other region of the world. Patten was arguing for a history curriculum focusing on British achievements and distinct British characteristics, rather than a curriculum which drew attention to the histories which Britain and other countries share.

The revised history orders (DFE, 1995a) do indeed emphasise British history. Within the programme of study at Key Stage 1, children are required to investigate: 'aspects of the way of life of people in Britain in the past beyond living memory' (DFE, 1995a: 74). Famous British men and women and British events are also included. At Key Stage 2, four out of the six units draw on British history for their content. However, there are some opportunities for moving beyond British history. Included within the key elements at Key Stage 1 is a requirement to teach: 'about aspects of the past through stories from different periods and cultures...' (DFE, 1995a: 75). At Key Stage 2, 'pupils should be given opportunities to study: ...aspects of the histories of England, Ireland, Scotland and Wales: where appropriate, the history of Britain should be set in its European and world context' (DFE, 1995a: 76).

We would urge that full account is taken of these requirements and that children's awareness of different countries' histories and cultures is developed. We need to bear in mind that the children now being taught in our primary schools will be the adult citizens of Europe in the next millennium. Some study of European history could help children appreciate the different cultures and heritages of which they are becoming a part. Britain is part of Europe and has an increasing complex role in world affairs. A broader historical approach would enable children to recognise the commonality as well as the differences between our traditions. The key idea of children as European and global citizens will be addressed further in Chapters 6 and 7.

Even if we accept a curriculum dominated by British history there still remain difficulties concerning the people and events to be studied. We turn now to consider some of these difficulties arising from the diversity of experiences emanating from the past.

*Diversity in history*

The trouble with history is it does not stop! There is an ever-increasing body of historical knowledge and range of historical enquiries. At the turn of the century the historian Lord Acton complained that the range of historical information threatened to turn the historian, 'from a man of letters into the compiler of an encyclopedia' (quoted in Carr, 1964:15). But history is not just a compilation of facts; the historian analyses the facts to present a particular picture of the past, as we have argued earlier.

Many recent historians have moved away from administrative and political history, so popular in the nineteenth century, and sought to examine the contribution which different groups in society have made to our history. This has resulted in many different stories and perspectives which have created a much richer and more varied view of the past. This diversity of British society is recognised within the history National Curriculum:

> They [pupils] should be taught about the social, cultural, religious and ethnic diversity of the societies studied and the experiences of men and women in these societies. They should be taught about the ideas, beliefs and attitudes of people in the past. (SCAA, 1994a:3)

In a minority report, McGovern, a member of the Dearing group advising SCAA on the history National Curriculum, has condemned this for carrying too much 'sociological baggage' (McGovern 1994). He argued that undue concentration on these elements would lessen the amount of time which could be spent on historical narrative and on the achievements and events which make British history so distinctive. The requirement that historical study should be introduced from a variety of perspectives – 'political; economic; technological and scientific; social; religious; cultural and aesthetic' (SCAA, 1994a:3) – has also been criticised:

> History, cannot in a school, be the medium for teaching culture or aesthetics. What are the English, foreign languages and art staffs for? If the scientists cannot manage a bit of history of science – always a useful shoehorn into the abstractions of physics of chemistry – are they doing their job properly? (Keegan, 1994)

In this writer's opinion children are seen very much as the consumers of knowledge; children acquire snatches of historical information from different lessons and are expected to make the links between them for themselves. However, one of the great strengths of history teachers would seem to be that they can take into account these different perspectives and can co-ordinate them to provide children with a broad understanding of a period of the past which includes the inter-relationship of all its different and varied features.

The diversity of history provides opportunities for looking at the varying roles in society undertaken by males and females, by different social classes and people from different ethnic backgrounds. We are not suggesting that these aspects should be viewed in isolation. They cannot be just tacked on to a study of history. Rather they should be seen as a part of history, enabling us to reach a greater understanding of the past.

For a long time women's contribution has been ignored. It is only 30 years ago that Ladybird published *Stone Age Man in Britain* (Du Garde Peach, 1961). Such a title appears to emphasise the contribution of men to history, at the expense of the other half of the population. Apart from a few very famous exceptions, such as Florence Nightingale and Queen Elizabeth I, women have been largely ignored. This omission can, however, provide an interesting point for discussion with children.

A group of 9- and 10-year-old children were working on a database concerning the history of flight. They had collected a lot of information but were puzzled that most of it concentrated on men's achievements. The following extract demonstrates how children tried to explain the omission of women and reveals a sophisticated awareness of how this might have come about (extracted from Howells, 1994):

> *Ruth:* I think women probably did more, but it was men that wrote about it so we don't know much about women.
> *Sylvia:* It's the same in lots of things you only ever have one or two examples about what women have done, but loads about what men have done.
> *David:* Perhaps the women weren't interested in flying.
> *Colin:* Those two Frenchwomen went up in the hot air balloon quite soon after it had been invented.
> *David:* But that might have been because they just knew the people.

Here the children were really trying to get to grips with difficulties of bias and the different interpretations resulting from deficiencies in the evidence. The group concluded their discussion and sought to redress the balance.

> *Sylvia:* If we include something about the women and what they did it would be better, it would show that women were interested in flight.

The local history units in the history National Curriculum provide opportunities for exploring the diversity of different communities. Collicott (1993), for example, has traced the history of individuals connected with the London Borough of Haringey and used these personal histories as starting points for making links with national and world history. In another article, Collicott (1992) has traced the black contribution to the Second World War and reminded us that about one-third of the soldiers fighting on the British side in the First and Second World Wars were from the Commonwealth and about one-eighth were black.

However, finding appropriate source material to resource these perspectives is not always easy. Collicott (1992) bemoaned the fact that few history books recognise the colonial contribution to the Second World War. Flanagan (1992) conducted an analysis of pictures in current history textbooks and noted that few books portrayed the very varied experiences of women during the war. But the difficulty in accessing relevant sources can offer opportunities for children to raise questions on why there is so little source material available and from such questions to consider what exactly constitutes history. Collicott (1992) posed the question, 'Why have war historians ignored the colonial contribution?' and concluded:

> It is a question of values. It is a question of which groups are considered important. Historians have their own value system and prejudices which are reflected in their writings. It is a prejudice which has to be challenged. Why has the black contribution been ignored has to be asked of children.' (Collicott, 1992:260)

Not only have different groups in society been omitted from history, but at times their particular contributions have been misrepresented. Returning to *Stone Age Man*, it is interesting to note how corn was first grown:

> Perhaps Quick Foot's wife, or some other woman, threw away some grass seeds beside the hut and noticed that they grew. Then she may have planted some more, and when these grew, cooked them in milk from the cows or goats, and made a sort of porridge. (Du Garde Peach, 1961:30)

Here present-day stereotypes of women's domestic roles have been dumped on to the Stone Age. There is little evidence to substantiate this account of the division of labour (earlier the men are described as busy making weapons and digging out canoes). Indeed in a subsistence economy this sharp delineation of roles would seem to be very unlikely.

Such stereotyping could be perpetuated in our schools if accounts of different people's experiences are excluded. Terry (1989) worked with two groups of children, who were both taught about the roles of Saxon and late medieval women and their contribution to society. One group of children was assessed before the female contribution was taught (Group A) and the second group was assessed following a specific input on the role of women (Group B). Terry's findings suggested that when the female experience was not taught, children imposed their current gender stereotypes on past societies and were also more likely to see historical groups in terms of male figures. When the children were asked to imagine they were a Saxon and to describe their day briefly, a much larger percentage of children from Group B identified with female roles and were able to project female experiences.

The recognition of the diversity of society recommended in the history National Curriculum is to be welcomed. Learning about the past helps children to develop a sense of their identity and their place in the world. Consequently, historical information which enables children to make their own personal links to establish their roots is important. Learning about the different histories of people in the past can extend children's under-standing of their own many and varied experiences and contribute towards a respect for those which are different.

This is not to suggest that children do not also need a broad framework against which these different histories can be set. Whatever group in society is studied still needs to be placed within the context of society at the time. Creating a balance between personal, local, national and global histories is a challenge for teachers and schools.

Having discussed some of the controversies surrounding the selection of parts of our past to be studied, we turn now to examine some of the ways in which children can learn about their past. We emphasise that history is about people and describe the range of sources which can be used to help children find out about the past.

## Finding the past: history is about people

*The legionary*

> It was approaching dusk and a family was exploring the remains of a Roman fort. Not all the fort had been excavated, but the outline of the walls and gatehouses was clearly visible rising from the trimmed grass. From the vantage point on the hill, the family looked down into the river valley below. In the twilight it was possible to imagine a Roman sentry on duty, nearly 2,000 years earlier, gazing down on the same scene. This thought was echoed by the 3-year-old in the party who declared, 'I'm a Roman legionary. This is where I lived and this is where my friend lived (pointing to two rooms, demarcated by little walls close to the gatehouse) and this is my gun'.

Here this 3-year-old has recognised one of the most important features of history – it is about real people who ate, slept, worked and played. These people had feelings and emotions too (in this example, the legionary had a friend). In his use of the past tense ('this is where I lived'), the child has recognised that this legionary lived in the past but he has also brought the legionary alive within his own imagination and within his own understanding of the present. We recognise the anachronism of the gun, but this child at the age of 3 was looking at the past through his own experience; he has used his current knowledge of military behaviour to reconstruct the past. This is exactly what, at a more sophisticated level, practising historians do.

This example serves as a powerful reminder of the effect which the environment can have on children's historical imaginations. Visits to historic sites and buildings can provide stimulating opportunities for children to respond to the past and to appreciate the threads which link the present to times long ago.

## An eighteenth century merchant's family

A class of 9- and 10-year-olds was learning about land transport, concentrating particularly on the eighteenth and nineteenth centuries. There were plenty of documentary and visual sources available, but the challenge was to make this source material meaningful and exciting for the children. The teacher conceived the story of the Macdonalds, an eighteenth century merchant family. One of the members of the family needed to make a journey to London. Brief biographies of the characters were created and their house located in a present day Bristol street.

Possible reasons for the journey were suggested and comparisons made with journeys which are made today. Source material was used for children to investigate the type of transport available and the condition of the roads. (The children did hope that their traveller would not drown and suffocate in the mud of a ditch, a mishap which had occurred to one unfortunate traveller in the sources used!) Pictures of old coaching inns provided useful information and the children were eager to read the table of tolls presented at old toll houses and to work out how much their carriage would be required to pay. A poster offering a reward for the capture of two highwaymen provoked much discussion. The children were provided with biographies of other highway robbers, including women such as Moll Cutpurse and used these to create their own 'Wanted for highway robbery!' posters.

Fortunately the Macdonald's coach was not robbed and finally reached London safely. The Macdonald's story provided a reason for engaging with source materials; it gave the children a purpose for their investigations and deductions and a context for their historical questions and solutions. Information was discounted and questioned as appropriate. Importantly too, it made the source material come alive, illustrated by this letter supposedly written by the father, John Macdonald, home to his family:

To my dear children, Bess and John,

The journey was dreadful and the weather was wet, windy and cold. We were attacked by a highway woman. I don't have much more money. I am half way to London. On the way I saw a man on horseback. One of the guards was blown off the roof of the carriage and into a muddy stream. We saw a coach that had turned over...

The children wrote their letters in ink and sealed them up with wax. The pens, ink, paper and sealing wax all added to the authenticity of the activity and to the children's enthusiasm.

The children's comments about the Macdonald family revealed how much they had enjoyed the activity. They had really entered into the story and were not sure whether the family was real or not. The episode really gripped one child's imagination and he kept on asking: 'How do you know? How do you know all this?' Surely these questions are the essence of what history is about.

*An airman in the Second World War: Frank Jackson's trunk*

Another way of facilitating story telling about real people in history is the provision of a collection of personal source items including artefacts as well as documents for whole class or group study.

A class of 10- to 11-year-old pupils was presented with a metal tin trunk containing a number of artefacts and personal documents which were brought back by a member of the Royal Air Force on his return from India and the East in 1946. The trunk still bore the inscription 'Not wanted on voyage', together with the RAF reference number and home address of its owner. Artefacts included part of his Air Force uniform, several small souvenir items brought from India including money, a gadget for rolling cigarettes and a cylinder of insect repellent. Photographs included those of the airman himself and several of his accommodation during his stay on location in India. There was also a letter sent to him by his young daughter. The documentation was extremely rich and included several note books in which the airman, evidently a maintenance engineer, had recorded details of how to repair damage to aircraft. There were tickets for entertainment provided for the troops overseas by the organisation ENSA, receipts for items purchased prior to leaving for India, inoculation records and many other pieces of personal documentation. For classroom use the items in the trunk had previously been divided into packets and each group of four or five children was allocated one packet to study.

Children first made a list of the items before going on to reconstruct as best they could the activities of LAC Frank Jackson, the airman to whom the trunk had belonged. They worked together sifting through the material and were then invited to tell Frank Jackson's war time experiences using the evidence available to them. Children were expected to listen to different opinions and to work out their own responses to the material. Working collaboratively enabled the children to share their ideas and to identify the most probable story of Frank Jackson. The following extract (Figure 2.3) illustrates one child's interpretation of the material.

> F.M. Jackson in India.
>
> Hae Mr Jackson, I am an areoplane man in World War II. At the moment I am fixing a plane that got shot down, so I am covering the blit holes with Perfex. After I wrote the inscrutions of it. I put the inscutions in a big black book. Then I got out a squared I had a little machine and I mean little you put the paper in first then the toebacks in then just turned it. I had a jacket it was not very big but I wore it so everyone knew I was English. We all had a book called For Your Guidance. That was for what to do and the stuff like that about the Airforce. I had a ticket for the Theater. It was in 30 Park Street in Calcutta where at that moment I was working. I started at nine. The only day I could go was on 15 January. I put all my stuff in the black box and set off to the boat. I needed a pastport it was not very big. When I got back to Lanshire I had to change my job and had to be a cleaner.

**Figure 2.3** Frank Jackson in India: a child's account

The three case studies above illustrate ways which permit children to enter imaginatively into other people's lives and to extend their own experiences. In this respect historical study can be seen to broaden our experiences, to look beyond the familiar and to take into account other perspectives and points of view:

Through history, pupils begin to explain their own experience in a larger context in which they encounter many aspects of human behaviour not readily observable in their own circle. (Blyth and Low-Beer, 1991:5)

## Resourcing a study of the past

These three examples drew on a range of historical sources to provide evidence for what people's lives in the past were like. We would now like to examine more fully the range of resources which are available to study our past. No one source can provide evidence for a complete picture of the past. Secondary sources such as books and TV programmes are important in providing narrative accounts and also contexts within which children can investigate actual primary sources effectively. Questions to be asked about sources will include; 'what do the sources tell us?' and also, 'what else would we like to know?' Opportunities to cross reference sources and to establish their validity need to be created.

For the Macdonald family's story, children used excerpts from diaries, court records and letters, and prints and paintings of transport at the time. The teacher prepared the sources and in some way therefore, could be seen to be influencing children's interpretations. These interpretations will vary according to the resources which are presented. Returning to Carr's (1964) analogy of fish, teachers will be responsible for the selection of most of the fish to be found swimming in the ocean, which children can then attempt to catch.

Using original documents is to be encouraged, although children may have difficulty in deciphering what has been written. When studying the Macdonald family the children worked from copies of the original 'Wanted for highway robbery!' poster and the list of tolls for the turnpike. They enjoyed trying to work out what some of the faint writing said and the tolls provided an added challenge in trying to work out the present-day equivalents for the sums of money involved. Help was needed with vocabulary, for example the descriptions of the different vehicles expected to pay tolls. However, it was worthwhile since the children were excited by looking at the actual documents and also used them as models in their own 'wanted' posters, offering guineas for rewards and dating events using Roman numerals. On other occasions transcripts of original documents describing the state of the roads were used. Although children could acquire information more easily about the roads, there was less enthusiasm generated than when copies of original documents were looked at.

Real excitement was created when an eighteenth-century leather-bound book was produced and the children were told that such a book might have been taken by the Macdonalds to read on their journey. The children were intrigued by the book's feel and smell. Some of the comments below indicate how the book sparked off their interest.

- It feels all mouldy.
- It smells old.
- How old is it?
- What do these letters mean? [Looking at the Roman numerals inside the front cover.]
- The paper feels all crinkly.
- Why do they do their letters like this? [Pointing to the f shaped letters representing the letter s.]
- It must be very valuable because it's so old.

The print proved fascinating. Anything the children wrote afterwards frequently included the archaic long 's', which they had read as 'f'.

The use of a range of historical sources to include documents, artefacts, pictures and photographs, music, people talking about the past, buildings and sites is advocated in the National Curriculum (DFE, 1995). The emphasis on source material encourages children to raise historical questions and to engage at first hand with historical material. In the past, work in history has often been criticised for too much colouring in and copying from textbooks (DES, 1978; HMI, 1989). The inclusion of sources in the key elements and level descriptions in the National Curriculum could be seen as a safeguard against such teaching. Critical analysis of source material, raising questions and looking for different solutions, establishing the value of source material for particular enquiries are all opportunities for children to work as real historians and to use sources as evidence to investigate the past.

## Children using sources

We turn now to discuss how children approach source material as evidence and describe some of their different interpretations. The children who examined the Macdonald family's book were able to recognise that the leather book was old since it matched their perception of what old should look like. But dating other objects is not always so easy. Children will often recognise things which are shiny as new. Signs of wear indicate age. Black-and-white photographs can affect children's ability to date objects and pictures accurately, with children assuming that coloured pictures are more recent (Harnett, 1993; Lynn, 1993). Perhaps children should be confronted with the old pair of shoes which have hardly been worn, the shiny pre-decimal penny, or a piece of Roman Samian pottery with its shiny red slip ware, so that some of their assumptions can be questioned. Children could take their own black-and-white photographs to help them realise that the present can be portrayed in such colours. These difficulties arise from children's lack of experience. But the suggestions made to help them overcome these misconceptions do emphasise the important role the teacher can have in extending children's ability to handle and date evidence.

Listening to children's reasons and explanations for their conclusions is important. Children might interpret the evidence in unforeseen ways. Donaldson (1978) suggests that young children do not always select the relevant details when problem solving, their reasoning can often stem from their immediate concerns. When reception infants were asked to sequence pictures of people from the youngest to the oldest, many placed a large picture of a baby as the oldest. Smaller pictures of adults were placed as younger. Here children might be utilising their knowledge of how their size increases as they grow older and consequently the big baby could be seen as the oldest. Closer observation of the picture and discussion focusing on different, age-relevant clues might enable these young children to alter their original choice of sequence.

Through talking and listening to children we can begin to realise some of the assumptions which they make as they interpret source material and develop their understandings of the past. Children do bring a tremendous amount of background knowledge to the learning situation; they will use this as they seek to make sense of fresh information. For example a group of infants working with an artefact rejected the suggestion that a leather-bound eighteenth-century book might be Roman because the Romans had books that were 'rolled up' with bits dangling down. This view was evidently informed by a recent Blue Peter programme featuring Pompeii.

An interesting activity is to ask children to write down all the things which they would like to find out about a particular source. Such an activity provides opportunities for children to raise historical questions and can also be used to help assess their historical understanding. A list of children's questions can be used as a basis for developing further historical enquiries. Research (e.g. Harnett, 1993; Lynn, 1993) would seem to suggest that intervention is important to help children extend their historical questioning. This enquiry-based approach is strongly supported within the key elements advocated in the history National Curriculum (DFE, 1995).

The sorts of activities which are provided in the classroom are also important in helping children to synthesise their existing knowledge. For example, asking children to debate, 'Were the Egyptians clever people?'

or asking them to rank information in order of importance requires that they review their existing knowledge and attach some value to it.


## Stories and history

Throughout the chapter we have emphasised that history is about people. Using source material can provide evidence of what life was like for people in the past. Listening to stories can provide more information and also opportunities for children to develop their awareness of the interpretive nature of history. The story which is told will be dependent on the sources available and also the viewpoint of the teller. We return to Carr's (1964) analogy of the fish in the ocean again; the fisherman chooses what part of the ocean he wants to fish in.

Evidently personal interest and significance will influence what is remembered and recounted. After a group of 6- and 7-year-old children were told the story of Dick Whittington, they were asked to recount it by drawing three pictures and labelling them with appropriate sentences (*see* Figure 2.4). The majority of the children began and ended their story in the same vein; their beginnings all recounted Dick Whittington's poverty and the endings all included his acquisition of wealth. The differences occurred in the middle part, revealing how different features of the story had appealed to the children. Some features were of more historical significance than others; some children mentioned that Dick was a merchant, whilst others were more interested in the tale of the cat and the rats and mice or the awful cook who had been so unkind to Dick in the version of the story retold to the children. It is interesting too that the way the story was told affected the children's accounts. As the storyteller described the rats in Dick Whittington's room, she elaborated further as she saw the children's interest was engaged, describing them clambering all over his bedclothes, over his arms and legs, over his pillow and even over his face! Such a detailed description evidently seized some of the children's imaginations and they included parts of it in their accounts. To make the story more interesting the storyteller had embroidered the facts and added more imaginary, though credible details. Yet it could be argued that this was moving the story even further away from the 'truth'.

Throughout time storytellers have sought devices to make their stories more interesting and to tell their point of view. Both Knight (1992) and Birley (1955) have demonstrated how some of our cherished historical characters have acquired additions to their life histories over periods of time. George Washington is probably most remembered for his reply, 'Father, I cannot tell a lie', on being questioned about cutting down the

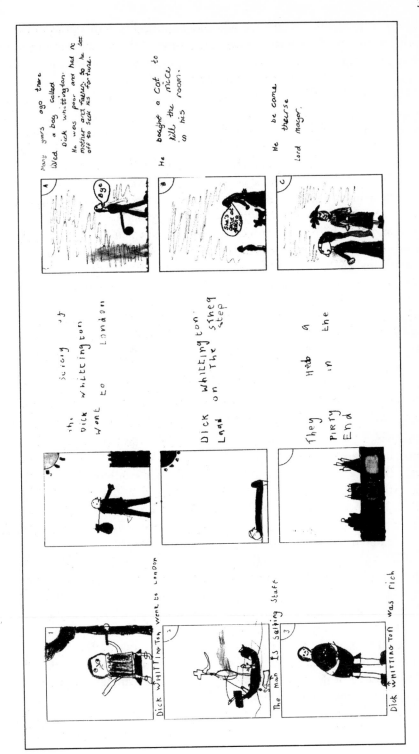

**Figure 2.4** The story of Dick Whittington as presented by 6–7-year-old children

cherry tree. Mention King Alfred, and burnt cakes will immediately spring to the minds of many people. Over time stories have changed and been modified. But because academic historians have found that these stories are unlikely to be true should we stop teaching them?

These stories have become part of an historical heritage. The elaborations of storytellers through time have created exciting and vivid images which can fire children's imaginations. Yet looking at how these stories have been assembled can also help children appreciate values held in past societies; what societies considered important and worth emphasis.

Interpretations continue today. The cartoon character Asterix, fights a guerrilla action against the Romans in the first century BC, and numerous cartoons and films incorporate the curse of the mummy's tomb. Children are confronted with many inaccurate images which they can utilise in investigations as to which parts might have some basis in historical fact and which parts might be purely fictional. A useful way of developing this awareness is to begin with looking at artists' reconstructions of past scenes and to examine how they have created an impression of the past. Artists' reconstructions are available at historic sites and children can be encouraged to differentiate the parts of these pictures which could have been based on evidence, for example the outline of the castle walls. This could be contrasted with other features such as people's faces or expressions, or animals which have been included to convey a particular atmosphere.

Recognition that the past can be represented in different ways is emphasised in the key elements for planning the history National Curriculum and in the level descriptions within the history attainment target (DFE, 1995). As children progress through the different levels they are expected to become increasingly critical, and to question both the validity of source material and how different interpretations might arise.

Finding discrepancies in primary and secondary sources can generate much excitement and enthusiasm. There is often immense surprise that texts in books might vary and that different sources might contradict each other. Pictures too might distort the truth. For example, portraits of Queen Elizabeth I in old age need to be set against the great propaganda machine of the Tudors. Elizabeth's concern over the image which she presented is evident and the Privy Council ordered in 1596 all portraits which were of 'great offence' to her to be destroyed (Strong and Oman, 1971:75).

We turn now to look at ways in which children are able to express their understanding of the past; in particular, at how they are able to organise their experiences within a temporal framework.

# A question of time

*Is it tomorrow today?*

This question from a 3-year-old encapsulates the difficulty which young children have in expressing their understanding of the passage of time. Tomorrow can never be reached, there are always successive tomorrows. Young children are inexperienced in the linguistic structures which can be used to convey our sense of the past and in selecting the most appropriate unit of time to use. Weeks and months are not very appropriate units to use when trying to record how long ago the dinosaurs lived! Thornton and Vukelich (1988) have attempted to map out children's progress in the acquisition of time-related concepts or skills. They provided a developmental framework demonstrating the relationship between the acquisition of historical and clock and calendar skills and concepts, and concluded that this relationship needed to be taken into account when introducing historical topics.

*Chronology – providing a temporal framework*

An awareness of the passage of time develops slowly as children experience talking about time and using the appropriate vocabulary. Initially, such vocabulary might include 'before' and 'after' and 'then' and 'now'. Personal time-lines can be used as a device to help children record the passage of time. Looking at events in their own lives provides instances for children to compare then (when I was a baby) and now. For older children, time-lines might include periods and different eras so that they can begin to use common historical terms such as Victorian, Roman, etc., and know their place in a chronological sequence. If a time-line becomes a normal feature of the classroom, whenever children acquire fresh historical information they can place it in context on their line. We saw in the opening chapter how the children used their classroom time-line to identify when the story of the Good Samaritan occurred.

The importance of placing experiences within the context of time was discussed earlier in the chapter. Personal histories can be set against a wider historical background. When the children were working with the objects from Frank Jackson's trunk, it was necessary for them to consider the circumstances in which British airmen were sent to India. The relevant context included the war against Japan and the landing of British troops in Burma. This information was mainly supplied to the class in the form of secondary sources, although the teacher also provided Japanese propaganda posters targeted on an Indian population whom they hoped might overthrow the British Raj in a general uprising.

The Macdonald family story was part of a more extended study on Land Transport and a time-line was constructed to enable children to place eighteenth-century developments within a broader context. Such a time-line illustrated the chronological sequence of different forms of transport; for example, the growth of canals immediately prior to the development of the railways, the development of public transport, buses and trams and the emergence of the private motor car. For periods of the time-line, transport continued in much the same way as before as in the case of travel on horseback or on foot. Ways of portraying this continuity had to be devised.

Temporal relationships can be demonstrated in other devices. A generation chart enables children to record different generations amongst their families and friends, and family trees can be useful for recording royal dynasties and other notable families.

Children's ability to fit historical information within a chronological framework develops through experience and is a continuous process. The examples of time-lines described here reveal ways in which children can deal with the abstract notions of time and can develop the linguistic skills necessary for them to express their growing understanding. Donaldson (1978) has argued that children's understandings of many abstract concepts are dependent on how the learning task is organised. This position contrasts with that of other researchers such as Hallam (1979), who claimed that children's historical understanding was dependent on their particular stage of development. Basing his research on a Piagetian framework, he argued that children's historical understanding was limited by their perception of time. He concluded that temporal and historical understanding were subject to developmental constraints.

## Conclusion

The case studies in this chapter reveal some of the difficulties in using a strict developmental framework when describing children's learning. Young children can deal with abstract notions, provided the context is appropriate and meaningful for them. Children's ways of working in history have been included since we recognise the importance of considering the learning situation from children's points of view. If we can recognise some of the potential difficulties which children might encounter, we will be well placed to design more suitable activities. We will return to this point in Chapter 8 when we discuss the value of role play and drama.

Returning to our initial question at the beginning of the book 'What is special about being human?', we would argue that we all possess a past, unique to ourselves. Fascination about this past stems from our earliest childhood. The past influences our lives, it shapes our identities, who and what we are now and what we will become in the future. Yet it is not a past held in isolation. We are social beings who interact with each other and influence the lives of others around us. Part of our past becomes part of other people's pasts too. Shared experiences are remembered and form part of our traditions. These traditions are important. Over the centuries we have learnt to record and to interpret them in many different ways, but they still remain our essential roots, and the part of our being which helps to anchor us firmly in the present.

# CHAPTER 3

## People and Place

This chapter is built around three 'case studies' – descriptions respectively of groups of children engaged in a variety of activities in school. The three cases have been selected to demonstrate the range of experience and understanding which constitutes geography. In the first, 5–6-year-old children are involved with maps, and questions of location. The second focuses on 10–11-year-old children considering elements of the physical environment. The third shows 8–9-year-old children thinking about people and place, in the context of a particular regional setting. As we note, geography extends beyond the humanities, but yet human concerns – concerns about the quality of life on earth – are at its heart.

We start by looking at younger children and the ways in which their relevant skills and knowledge develop.

### CASE STUDY

#### 1: Infants drawing their journeys to school

Five Year 1 children are sitting with two student teachers around a large-scale map of the local area, an inner urban part of Bristol. One of the students says:

What we're going to do today is draw a journey of our way to school. Can anyone tell me about the way they come to school?

One child responds:

I go out of my house and I go down the road and I pass lots of traffic-lights and I go straight down and I go up a road and then I come to school.

Another child says:

I stand out my back door and I go through my garden over the wall and I only pass some houses and some gates.

A third child says:
When I walk I pass a post-box. When I walk I pass a bus stop as well. After the bus stop I see the post-box.

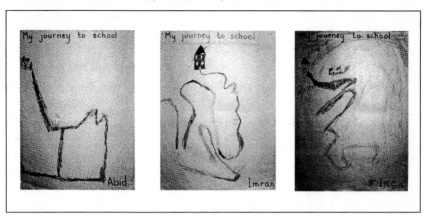

**Figure 3.1** Journeys to school

In spite of encouragement the two other children find difficulty in describing their journeys to school, although their responses indicate that they do understand what is being discussed. After further discussion with the students all five children proceed to draw a representation of their various routes to school (*see* Figure 3.1). None of them have any writing on them, but they all include a strong linear element, a road and sometimes a path, with twists and turns and various pictorial representations of gates, trees, houses, traffic-lights, pillar-boxes and the like. These are essentially 'topological' diagrams, which show the connections between the key features of their journeys in the children's minds.

To some adults it could appear misleading to call these route drawings maps, because their scale is variable and some of the representations are drawn with a horizontal view, others from an aerial perspective. Nevertheless, they clearly indicate an early skill in map making and, to follow a well-established field of study in geography, may accurately be described as mental maps. The creation of the maps also led to a significant increase in the amount of discussion and the confidence with which the children could talk about their journeys (*see* O'Hare, 1987).

These children are clearly becoming geographers. From the first time that an infant moves she or he is beginning geographical development. The skills which later come to be seen as geographical, such as mapping, navigating and locating – may be seen to originate in very early childhood experiences.

What the case study above also demonstrates, however, is that the range of skills varies quite considerably. One of the children who did not offer a verbal account, nevertheless drew a very detailed graphic account. The fifth child, who did not speak much, had in fact started attending the school that very day, having just moved into the area. She too was able, given the opportunity to draw, to give a detailed account of significant features of her journey – a journey she had possibly made only once.

It may be helpful to identify the key terms and ideas which underlie this discussion. Firstly there is the very idea of a map. We may take a map to be a symbolic representation, with a particular schematic projection. Children are likely to start, as we have seen, from a topological understanding, that is they will describe the connectedness of places or things. This is why the use of picture/maps which represent routes and journeys (as in the case study above) at an early stage is so effective. It is also why young children often find it difficult to present the imagined aerial view. Even when encouraged to look down on a desk top with a number of objects on it, many children do not find it easy to draw the objects' outlines onto a piece of paper. Actually placing the objects onto a piece of paper and then drawing around them can be helpful though.

But a map, as well as being symbolic, is also selective. One of the difficulties for children derives from this fact. When asked to draw a plan of say a desk top the result will often include items which the adult may consider unnecessary or irrelevant, for example some stains or scribbles on the desk's surface. Until purposes and functions of mapping are understood it is unlikely that a child's mapping activities will consistently select relevant features. The same process is true of the reading of pictures (*see* Harnett, 1993). When asked to describe a picture, children tend to give a very full and detailed account but do not attach significance to particular features systematically.

The other key idea which is implicit in the case study is that of place. What is a place? Is it 'my house', an airport, Bristol or the Mendips? Place can be specific with a fixed location on the earth's surface (*see* below) or generic like deserts or sweet shops. What is common in either case is that a place may be ascribed a set of characteristics

Children's conception of near and far is also important here. It relates closely to concepts of scale. An interesting activity with any child or group of children is to draw four concentric circles on a large sheet of paper and ask them to name places in each ring which are, respectively, near to me, quite near, far and very far away. As well as revealing children's understandings of these terms, the exercise also reveals children's knowledge about relative location. (We return to the question of distant places later in the chapter.)

Other activities which are useful both in assessing and developing mapping skills of young children include the provision of play mats of road networks, creating models of buildings and on a base plan. A number of children's books have maps in them (e.g. *Winnie the Pooh, The Village of Three Corners*) and a number of stories include journeys which children can create maps to represent (e.g. *Rosie's Walk, The Jolly Postman, Each Peach Pear Plum*). Figure 3.2 shows how one 5 year old conceived the walk that Rosie took.

**Figure 3.2** Rosie's walk – a child's view

The extent to which mapping should be seen as a 'basic skill' has been argued out over the years. Indeed a number of writers have suggested that 'graphicacy' is as fundamental as literacy, numeracy and oracy (and some would say physiognomacy) (*see* Boardman, 1983; Proctor, 1985). Certainly children who have an awareness of spatial relationships and abilities to represent and manipulate space and spaces are likely to be children who are becoming independent learners.

A location is a fixed place and the idea that each location is indeed fixed, is, in Piagetian terms, a form of conservation. People and most features to be found in the landscape are not actually fixed, especially when a long time span is considered. One idea then which children may start to grasp in KS1 is that landscapes do indeed evolve, whether it be through the actions of humans or through rivers or the weather.

Our second case study focuses on one aspect of physical geography; but as we shall see, children tend to take a humanistic approach to it.

CASE STUDY

## 2: Volcanoes with 10- and 11-year-old children

Two teachers, Sue Pritchard and June Saunders, are working with a group of six Year 6 children. The children had done some work on volcanoes and earthquakes in their previous year. Sue wanted to continue their work on this topic but needed first to establish how familiar they were with this subject, which at the time was part of Geography Attainment Target 3 – physical geography – in the National Curriculum. In other words, Sue wished to assess the children's knowledge and understanding of volcanoes and earthquakes.

Working with June, Sue began by asking the children what they know about volcanoes and earthquakes. She also produced a piece of rock, which was volcanic in origin. This was followed by using other resources, including viewing part of a school's television programme on earthquakes and volcanoes, and then a drawing of a volcano to show different features above and below the surface.

With Sue taking the lead in asking many of the questions, June compiled a floorbook as a means of recording the children's knowledge of this topic.

Sue and June were greatly impressed, and indeed surprised, by the extent of the children's knowledge. Early talk was about what it is like inside a volcano. The children were fully aware of the nature of magma (molten rock).

– It is called lava.
– It is like tar off the road – hot and runny.

The relationships between the plates found in the earth's crust, earthquakes, and volcanoes were also appreciated by many of the children. The following are snatches of what the children said as they talked between themselves about Vesuvius.

– When Vesuvius erupted, the lava flowed down.
– There were folds in the earth – plates.
– This is where the rocks rubbed over each other.
– There is the ring of fire.

This shows, despite some inaccuracies, how the children did make an association between those phenomena which we (as geographically informed adults) might know as tectonic plates (i.e. major solid rafts of rock which underlie continental landmasses and the oceans), earthquakes and volcanoes, and the 'ring of fire'. This is the Pacific rim where instability in the earth's crust is often manifest in earth movements, tremors and re-adjustments in the Pacific coastal regions. One child also showed a good understanding of what lies beneath the surface

# Features of volcanoes

You find geysers near volcanoes.

The outer core is more solid.
The inner core is liquid.

Magma becomes lava.

Volcanoes happen along fault planes.
When the plates move apart the magma can escape.
Melted rock comes out of the volcanoes.

Volcanoes can be found in Iceland.

The mantle is like plasticine - it moves.

Vesuvius and Etna are the names of volcanoes.
Krakatoa. The Ring of fire, in the Pacific.

There might have been volcanoes in the Lake District,
    or Scotland.
There might have been volcanoes in the Isle of Wight.

**Figure 3.3** Features of volcanoes

of the earth's crust, and of the nature of the interior of the earth.
*Sue:* If I were a giant saw, and cut the earth in half, what would
be inside?
*Hugh:* An inner core.
*Sue:* Would it be liquid or solid?
*Hugh:* Liquid.
*Sue:* And the outer core?
*Hugh:* Solid
The following is the record (floorbook) of the children's
statements and ideas on this topic as recorded by June when
they were asked to say what they knew about this topic. The
floorbook demonstrates very effectively how the children's
attention was caught by the subject of volcanoes. This then

helped them to develop basically sound ideas not only of volcanoes, but also of the role of plates in the earth's crust. These are subject to movements, which in turn give rise to earthquakes, and help to release underground reserves of magma. This is the essence of volcanoes and of volcanic activity. The text reads as follows:

Dormant volcanoes are sleeping.

Shield volcanoes – some have the top chopped off.

Different rocks come out of volcanoes.

Some volcanic rocks float on water.

Describing the rock sample:

It has got a high density.

It is rough and sharp.

The rock looks like an Aero bar.

It's got lots of bubbles.

The illustration (Figure 3.3.) summarizes some of the other comments and descriptions offered by the children. We can recognize the breadth of interest and of understanding that they showed in this topic.

There are of course some inaccuracies in some of the points put forward here, for example the Isle of Wight is not noted for volcanic activity, even in the distant geological past. There is probably also some confusion between shield volcanoes, and those which have had their 'top chopped off' – perhaps calderas were what the children had in mind. These are formed when massive explosions remove much of the upper cone of volcanoes. Shield volcanoes arise from lava which flows great distances before cooling.

Seemingly more prosaic questions were:

– Which was the first volcano to erupt?

– Which country or continent has the most active or dormant volcanoes?

– How long does a volcano stay active for?

Two other questions showed that children were able to extrapolate some of these key ideas, and to make relationships between other phenomena:

– Does lava come out of earthquakes?

– Why doesn't the moon have any active volcanoes?

These questions raise some sophisticated notions. They also demonstrate the links between physical geography and science.

Overall there was evident enthusiasm, as well as much knowledge retained from the children's earlier work on this topic. It would seem that the massive amounts of energy, the potential for disaster, and the threat to life were among the aspects arousing interest in the children. The threat to people, and the uncertainty of these eruptions were mentioned in some of the questions posed by the children for further investigation at the end of the first lesson.

These questions included:

– Has anyone stood in boiling lava – and lived to tell the tale?
– Which volcano has killed the most people?
– Which is the biggest volcano (eruption)?
– How can we tell when earthquakes and volcanoes are going to happen?
– Which country has most earthquakes each year?

Thus, even though the topic is essentially a physical one, children's interest in it and understanding of it is motivated very much by humanistic concerns. Volcanoes can stimulate great interest because they do connect with people's lives. They can also fire the imagination as shown by the 6-year-old boy who combined an accurate geomorphological description of volcanic activity with a solemn explanation that this was all brought about by the dragon who lived underneath it. Plate tectonics are significant because they have shaped the lands on which human life has evolved and now lives.

We can also note in passing how important is the role of the teaching style in providing opportunities for positive assessment of what children know and can achieve. The teachers were consciously seeking to ascertain what children knew on this topic, and they provided an open and supportive situation in which children could feel free to express, and indeed enjoy, themselves.

In our third case study we explore the relationship between people and place in greater depth as we witness work within environmental and human geography. The central theme was that of people and 'distant' places.

CASE STUDY

### 3: South Africa – people, and a distant place

In this classroom scene, 8–9-year-old children in Pilning Primary school on the fringe of north Bristol are sitting in a circle on a carpet. With them is their teacher, Chris Howard, and two student teachers, Tina Hickman and Heidi Chiswell, who are in the second year of their 4-year B.Ed. course. This is the last Monday in a sequence of seven in which they have come in to work with the children, alongside the class teacher. They are using a floorbook as a vehicle for discussion, and as a way of assessing children's learning. The children, recalling their experiences, are discussing some of their initial perceptions and changed images of Africa, and of people living in African countries. The discussion moves on to South Africa and questions of human rights and social justice.

During the previous few weeks, the children had been developing their knowledge and understanding about people and places in Africa. This work was linked to the end-of-term school concert in which the children would be engaged in music and dance. Initially working at a continental scale, and using a map of Africa, they had considered physical aspects, and different environments such as desert, sub-tropical grasslands, and tropical rainforests. Attention was given also to people, and to elements of social and economic geography. Topics included different types of work, transport and other means of communication, buildings, and urban and rural contrasts.

They had then moved on to focus more specifically upon one country – South Africa. Ideas of place and places, ideas too of people in those places and their complex social relationships were developed. The daily lives and experiences of people affected by apartheid were central to talking and learning about the geography of the country. Key resources used included maps, photographs, cotton fabrics with traditional designs, and a video programme from a lower secondary schools TV series. It featured children talking about their experiences of living in South Africa, and images of selected localities.

Several questions which may come to mind include:

- is it not more appropriate for primary children, especially 8-year-olds, engaged in a geographical study of people and place in the wider world, to focus on a place at the scale of a locality, rather than a country or continent?;
- surely the moral questions likely to be raised in a consideration of apartheid are too complex to enter into worthwhile and meaningful geographical work with 8-year-olds?;
- does not the fact that the video film was aimed at secondary school age children mean that it would be 'over the heads' of these younger children?

These are questions to which we will return below.

The following are some extracts of classroom discussion, which although in this instance were strongly teacher co-ordinated, did encourage children to express their own ideas and views. Very nearly all the extracts offered are in the order in which they occurred during the course of the lesson.

*Children's images of the continent of Africa: of landscapes, people and place*

Chris Howard, class teacher, sets the scene and introduces the activity to the children.

*Teacher:* We started off 6 weeks ago...put your brain in gear. We will use a big piece of paper to write down. Remember we all worked very hard. Who can remember the first thing we did?... To see what you already knew – or thought you knew – the things we knew about Africa. It didn't matter if you were not absolutely sure – but we wanted you to give us all your ideas before we did any work.

To get a picture of images of the African continent the children had when beginning the topic they were encouraged to recall their initial perceptions and ideas of people and place. The African continent was the starting point before moving on to consider South Africa.

Children responded initially by posing their images as questions: Did they have schools? Did they have buildings? Did they have cities? Did they have cars?

Chris went around the class inviting children to speak in turn. As children spoke, she would make a response, usually affirming their question, and recording it on the large piece of sugar paper – the 'floorbook'. This ensured that all children would be able to participate, and all their contributions could be valued. It also enabled her to assess some of the children's learning. As children got further into the activity, some were offering statements of individual understanding, rather than posing questions.

*Angela:* Did black people have houses?
*Gill:* I didn't know they had shops.
*Tor:* I thought Africans lived in mud huts.
*Lalit:* They did not get much to eat.
*John:* I thought Africa was all deserts.

It is interesting to see just how strongly some of the widely recognized biased and inaccurate images of people and place in the African continent were held in the minds of the children, images such as the absence of buildings, cars, and living in mud huts (they are almost stereotypes of stereotypes, if that is possible). They began by thinking of contrasts to their experience of their own world around them, starting with schools, followed by other familiar features of their urbanized world.

It is also interesting to see how similar are the children's African images when compared with children in other studies (*see* Wiegand, 1992:92). These early ideas of place also have a strong visual or scenic element to them, as opposed to more abstract notions of how people live and interact.

> The children were then invited to consider how their perceptions have changed. Some of the responses confirmed how their perceptions had changed, complementing the revised images which have been noted above: that there are cities; there are buildings, schools, cars, farming and food crops in many parts of Africa. Sometimes a child might state what he or she had learnt, and then be prompted by Chris to say how that understanding had been developed.
>
> *Leila:* I thought there was only one airport in Africa – to start with, now I know there is quite a few of them, and quite a lot of travellers as well Miss.
>
> *Teacher:* How did you find that out?
>
> *Leila:* Well when I was reading the book you gave us there was a picture, and among the pictures a picture of airplanes and airports.

This is a simple illustration of children enquiring and using evidence, or sources, to find out and establish some things for themselves, and not always relying upon direct teacher input for information. Tina and Heidi had previously told the children that they wanted them to 'act like detectives, and to find out what you can from looking at pictures and photographs' of selected African scenes of people and place.

> It was shown by comments from other children that varied landscapes and environments were now acknowledged; that there was not one simple homogeneous landscape or environment in Africa. There were:
> - shanty towns
> - shanty towns where the poor people live
> - dry parts in Africa
> - some forest...and grasslands
> - I knew they had cities – I didn't know they had big ones
> - I was surprised to see all those skyscrapers.

As the children continued to recall their thoughts of what they had learnt, and how their perceptions of Africa had changed, they moved on to thinking about the people. What did they do? How do they live? How did they get on with their neighbours? Again the natural opportunities which occur in geography for children to think about questions in relation to 'what is special about being human?' were illustrated. One basic quality of being human is to affirm that there is not only such a thing as society, but that we all depend upon each other to a greater or lesser degree.

Chris Howard was able to remind the children of this concept of interdependence – that as humans we all rely on each other – following a discussion leading through factories, chocolate and burger-bars.

*Teacher:* I was just thinking, with all the things we like to drink – coffee, tea, hot chocolate – all the main things that go into those drinks do not grow in this country. We have to buy them, and they are all grown in Africa. Really if they did not grow those crops in Africa, we would not be able to have all these drinks.

Part of this discussion showed how the teacher was challenging some of the stereotypical images that children might well have of people and places in Africa. Ideas of working in factories, Coca-cola, the eating of chocolate, and having access to burger-bars do not sit easily with mud huts, deserts, and malnutrition. She is also taking the opportunity to deepen children's understanding of the key concept of interdependence: how we all rely on each other to provide for many of our needs and desires.

Commercial geography was a major strand within geography in Britain in the period between the two world wars. With an emphasis upon the role of trade between countries, and the rote learning of imports and exports, it typified a strongly descriptive approach to geographical study. Regional geography comprised accounts, country by country, listing relief and climatic background, before moving on to describe features of human geography and of economic activity. These commonly included statistics about trade: imports and exports of raw materials and finished goods, along with tons of minerals produced – all to be paraded in front of the glazed eyes of the passive pupils. For many of us growing up and going to school in the United Kingdom the role of tropical and sub-tropical producers of foodstuffs and raw materials as providers of our Western needs and wants went unquestioned.

It was probably the lingering influence of this fact-laden commercial geography which influenced Dame Angela Rumbold's view of what would be appropriate for schoolchildren in England and Wales today. While holding office as a junior minister of education prior to the publication of the National Curriculum Geography statutory orders she was asked what children should learn in geography. She replied that they should learn important things such as the names of the different currencies used in European countries. 'Trivial pursuits' curriculum content (Galton, 1995) such as this is beloved of right-wing politicians. Presumably it would underpin a monetary outlook upon the world, and, while learning such mind-numbingly boring facts, children would be in little danger of developing an enquiring approach to real issues of people, place and environment. Further, very little light would be thrown in a positive fashion on what is special about being human.

Key ideas such as mutual support, interdependence and 'fair trade' underpin the approaches promoted in more recent times as part of Development Education, and of World Studies (*see* Fisher and Hicks, 1985; Pike and Selby, 1988; Steiner, 1994) as well as humanist geography. In these approaches children, as well as adults, are encouraged to recognise how much we depend in our daily lives upon the efforts and products from people near and far. These approaches contrast strongly with the more traditional eurocentric values which characterised so much earlier geography teaching.

Commonly there are three major study emphases identified in geography. They are:

- location or spatial patterns;
- areas or regions; and
- people and environmental relationships (Haggett, 1983:6).

These elements of geography are summarised in Figure 3.4. Questions of people and their interrelationship with different aspects of their environment occurred naturally at several points during this lesson on Africa. This exploration of problems of food supply in some parts of the continent is one such discussion:

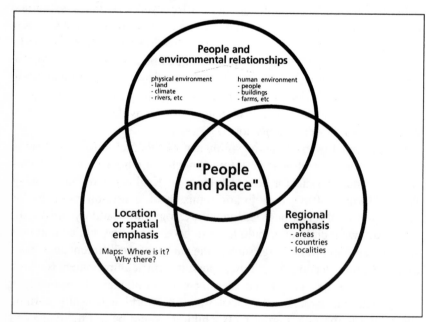

**Figure 3.4** Elements of geography

*Teacher:* What makes some people in some parts of Africa go short of food?

*Jane:* They can't grow certain things in parts of Africa. Seeds can't grow.

*Teacher:* Seeds can't grow...what do you need?

*Tony:* Sunshine.

*Teacher:* Sunshine – another thing which stops people getting their food – what's that? Steven?

*Steven:* Wars.

*Teacher:* Good boy, that is something that we can do something about – stop the fighting.

*Teacher:* What else?

*Gloria:* Water – make special pumps.

In this discussion, children were expressing their understanding of people and environmental links. There is an awareness of people interacting with the physical elements of their environment (e.g. the need for sunshine and water supply) and this could reflect previous learning from home or infant science lessons with growing cress. There is also reference to the effects of the social, or people-made environment, with political factors such as fighting being identified as a major influence upon how people live, work and play.

We can recognise how much these children had developed their knowledge and understanding of people and place in the African continent. There remain many gaps and inaccuracies, but nevertheless their enthusiasm, their interest, and their ability to reason about relationships between people and environment were evident. They also showed an ability to empathise in various ways. Overall, this case study illustrates a number of successful and valuable learning experiences about the 'geography of Africa'.

*Children's understanding of the social geography of South Africa*

The value-laden nature of geography is also unquestionable when key ideas in human geography about how people live and work are discussed. On the one hand simple and uncontentious values about favourite foodstuffs can be freely expressed. Children enjoy talking about food, as was shown during this lesson. It is also a topic which gives opportunities for all children of whatever ability to participate and provide a viewpoint. On the other hand human geography can involve children in more critical questions and issues: for example, how some groups of people are denied land rights, or have unequal access to varied resources. Some infant children, as well as juniors, have shown the ability to have some understanding of the moral issues involved in aboriginal land rights in Australia – a topic developed in books such as that by Fisher and Hicks (1985).

Chris Howard led the discussion to focus more strongly upon one country – South Africa. The theme which emerged strongly from the children's comments was how people relate to each other – people/people relationships, rather than simply people/environment links. This illustrates again how geography can provide a natural forum for children to consider questions of 'what is special about being human?'. Social geography has a particular emphasis upon the spatial organisation of society, and on how different social groups have unequal access to resources of many kinds.

Many of their ideas about people and of place in South Africa reflected some earlier notions which children had advanced about other countries in Africa. However, many of the crucial injustices of apartheid were not lost on the children. They showed a good knowledge of 'shanty towns', and of the pressures under which black south Africans lived – 'shanty towns – burying cardboard boxes in the ground because bulldozers would come and raze it'.

Interdependence on a global scale was again explored:

*Mary:*     ...cold countries they cannot grow...in hot countries you can get ...we can share each others food.
*Teacher:* Good – what do we call it?
*John:*     Sharing?
*Teacher:* Yes, or another name.
*Richard:* Swapping?
*Teacher:* Or trade. Trading; what do you think we should pay them?
*Joan:*     A fair price.

We can appreciate here that there was a little more teacher-direction in eliciting ideas and responses. Nevertheless the children suggested, without prompting, the possibility of sharing; also the idea of a 'fair price' was for some of them a key principle in whatever should be the payment. These 8- and 9-year-old children recognise principles of fairness, and of the need to share. This response of children to social situations of fairness or not being fair can commonly occur in classrooms. It is also touched on in Chapter 5 when 9- and 10-year-old children were discussing those who are homeless.

The indignant claim 'It's not fair' is probably to be heard daily in every primary classroom in relation to a wide range of perceived injustices – usually against the person voicing the claim. The concepts and feelings embodied in this claim lie at the heart of issues arising in moral education, religious education and 'education for citizenship'. When children respond to some social interaction and decide that 'it's not fair', they are also developing further insights into the question 'what is special about being human?'.

Many children went on to describe how they thought people should act towards each other in a mixed community like South Africa. It is evident in the remarks of many that they can put themselves into the position of black children, and know how they would feel if they had been discriminated against in the same way. Again this is an opportunity for the teacher to help them develop their understanding of what is special about being human. The video lesson had portrayed shanty towns, as well as a beach where bathing facilities were supposed to be restricted to white people only. Children were able to recall vividly much of what they had seen, and were keen to express their ideas and feelings about them.

The patent injustice of the black family being moved off the beach was apparent to the children:

> It should not only be for whites – they are not allowed to play with each other.

Children advocated tolerance and understanding between those of different ethnic groups:

> If they are going to live, they should get on together if only whites and blacks could share the same beach.

Again the basic principle of 'fairness' was argued for black families as well as white people. Children drew contrasts between 'some places, people living in very nice places – bungalows, with water' and the 'shanty towns' with 'houses of corrugated iron, and of cardboard'. One child summed up her solution to these observed inequalities between different social groups: 'They should all be fair', thus implying a sharing of wealth and resources generally.

The previous week Tina and Heidi had developed a discussion of these key ideas about justice and citizenship with the children. The children produced their own 'children's charter' which summarised their collective feelings about such issues. The recommendations that they made had pride of place on the classroom door, and are illustrated in Figure 3.5.

Listening to the discussion it was apparent that for many of these 8- and 9-year-old children there was no question that colour of skin, or other indications of ethnic grouping, should provide any basis for apartheid or any other crude distinctions to be drawn between people, and how they are treated. These ideas were exchanged readily between them, and some children showed a remarkable awareness of the difficulties and problems involved. It was not a simple matter to get everybody to live together,

## The children's charter

1) Everyone should have clean water and good food.
2) Everyone should have equal chances to do what they want.
3) Everyone should have the chance to be in the government, no matter what their colour, or whether they are male or female.
4) Laws should be fair.
5) People from different cultures should mix together. Then there might be fewer wars.
6) Everyone should have an equal education.
7) People should share and take care of each other.
8) People should share and take care of each of each other.
9) Freedom and peace for everyone.
10) Any more ideas...?

**Figure 3.5(a)** The children's charter

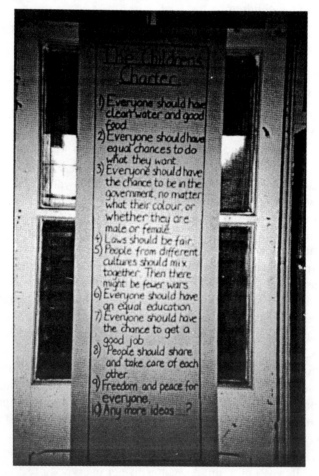

**Figure 3.5(b)** The children's charter

even though that was the ideal they advocated:

*Rebecca:* They should mix. They want to mix.

*Pete:* In the mix-up there will need to be a lot of understanding.

*Lara:* The boy [in the film] said, 'they do not see us as black. They think of us as animals....'

*Clare:* We all are humans – what is the difference? They are a different colour...just darker skin.

*Teacher:* Mo – what do you think ought to happen now?

*Mo:* They ought to live together.

*Catherine:* I am white, and I want the blacks and whites to live together.

*Teacher:* Do you think all the white people would agree with you?

*Peter:* No.

*Teacher:* Why not?

*Peter:* 'Cause the whites have done horrible things over the years. Why should you make friends with them?

We can at this stage recall the questions posed at the beginning of this case study, relating to:

(a) Should geographical study in primary classrooms concentrate upon areas at the scale of a locality, rather than a country?

(b) Is a topic such as apartheid too complex for primary children to consider?

(c) Can resources for adult or secondary school age be successfully used with primary children?

These excerpts from the latter part of the lesson show that these children had successfully engaged with a video resource prepared for secondary age children, and the topic of apartheid and related issues. They had been able to empathise to a worthwhile extent with families, black and white, in South Africa. It has been generally accepted in the past that primary children would normally study localities, rather than a whole country. Nevertheless these children talking showed that there are times when they can gain useful insights onto features of physical and human at a national scale.

In concluding the lesson Chris talked to the children about how we relate to people we may think are different to us. She said 'Make sure you treat them just exactly in the same way as you like to be treated yourself.'

We can note that this 'treat others as you would like them to treat you' is a central tenet of many major faith traditions (this is explored further in

Chapter 4, *see* pp.74–76). It also concerns developing the quality of empathy – putting yourself in the position of others (*see* Chapter 8). In the New Testament it was the lawyer, considering the teaching 'love your neighbour as yourself' and seeking clarification of who his neighbour might be, who prompted Jesus to tell the story of the Good Samaritan.

In the classroom activity just described, these 8–9-year-old children have been involved in the study of people and place at a national scale and at a continental scale. It was evident that children (a) already had a large number of images of Africa before beginning classroom-based study, and (b) they deepened their knowledge and clarified their understanding in many ways regarding people and place. The emphasis was upon children learning more about the lives and lifestyles of real people. Their responses show how they can get involved and are able to appreciate many aspects of how people relate to each other, and how they use the resources provided within their environment.

It is interesting to see how when studying distant places, children might start – like adults – by identifying those features which contrast with their own locality. Aspects of the physical geography ('deserts', 'jungles', 'open spaces') were readily suggested alongside social and cultural attributes (e.g. types of housing, absence of schools, foods). However, there are opportunities to see the ways in which there are many similarities which are shared between peoples who might happen to live in very different social and physical environments. Many geographers, as well as other teachers, have long argued for children to be drawn to consider these similarities rather than only highlight the differences. There is the attraction for us all in studying the exotic and the unusual but the dangers of overemphasis in the (geography) lesson need to be guarded against.

It was also clear in the discussion how readily children can empathise, and put themselves in the position of others. What was not evident in that particular lesson was an expression of racist feelings. In a previous lesson a child had advanced the question 'My Dad says "why can't they all go home to their own country?"' Such questions require a positive response from teachers, and this class discussion illustrated ways in which such responses were being made.

A vital concept for children to understand as part of their geographical education is that of interdependence. This notion was illustrated in the context of supply and demand for foods, and the exchange of raw materials between countries. Children made other suggestions about the exchange of knowledge and of technological expertise. It could be seen too in the ideas expressed by the children when talking about blacks and whites in South Africa, that there is the need to recognise interdependence

between members living within the same community. 'They should mix –
they want to mix', in the words of Rebecca; and Catherine stated 'I am
white, and I want the blacks and whites to live together.'

*Geography as a vehicle for promoting anti-racist understanding in the classroom*

Teachers are now much more aware of the need to avoid bias and
stereotyping than was the case 10 or 20 years ago. Many of us have grown
up with pictures of 'other peoples' which often are not only biased and
distorted, but represent negative images of them. Certain popular
newspapers still offer the crude xenophobic sentiments, which can only
pander to the racist inclinations which lie just below the surface – if not
actually observable – of the attitudes of very many of us. This tends to be
particularly true when it comes to children's perceptions of 'the
developing world' (Graham and Lynn, 1989).

One of the most important contributions of the humanities teacher in
primary schools is to use these opportunities to try to help children
develop a more balanced and informed way of looking at people and
place. In so doing this can be part of an anti-racist process, which is
central to children growing up to take their place as responsible citizens
in a civilised society. We saw above how opportunities were taken to
present positive images and to challenge inaccurate perceptions held by
children. This was done in a natural and non-threatening way. Indeed the
whole approach was that of recognising that we all start from a particular
base of knowledge and experience. We can then think about how we have
changed our knowledge, viewpoints and understandings in the light of
discussion, enquiry and reflection. For children the style of teaching and
learning in this classroom facilitated exchange of views, knowledge and
findings between children themselves, and was not simply a case of
learning only from the inputs of the class teacher.

Images of people and places which are unduly biased, can support the
promotion of stereotypes. It has been argued that stereotypes have four
important functions. Wiegand (1992:80), drawing on Tajfel's work,
describes them thus:

(a) A cognitive function, which allows us...to make sense of a mass of
    incoming information....
(b) A value preserving function...Categorizing people's personal character-
    istics usually [involves values]...
(c) An ideologizing function. Stereotypes seem to have been created in the
    past to explain complex and stressful social events, particularly those
    involving gross actions against minority groups....

(d) A positive differentiation function...People identify themselves as members of a category and it becomes a useful defence mechanism to be able to allocate others to categories too.

Stereotyping therefore can easily shade into racism. Although research has demonstrated the development of racial awareness or ethnic identity at a very early age (as young as 3), research also suggests that stereotyping as a process tends to take a real hold of young people's discourse during their teenage years. However the stereotyping which takes hold then is in some senses an exaggerated form of the generalising which children engage in from a much younger age. Therefore the role of the primary teacher can be seen to be critical in helping children to understand the nature of generalisation and what it is that turns it into stereotyping.

In 1985 the Geographical Association set out a Statement on Antiracism (Walford, 1985). This is as applicable in teaching 5-year-old children as it is in teaching undergraduates. Amongst other items the Association affirmed its intention:

to encourage all geography teachers
(a) to consider what forms of behaviour might justifiably be regarded as racist
(b) to develop their own and their pupils' awareness of racism – both in the textbooks and materials they use, and in their own and their pupils' contributions to lessons
(c) to condemn such racism
(d) to consider how geographical education may best seek to counter racism.

It serves us all well to be sensitive and to recognise ways in which we can easily take things for granted where offence can be caused to those of ethnic minority groups. In the supermarket the tea packet with the picture of the woman smiling brightly as she goes about the laborious task of picking the tea is now avoided. This is since a colleague pointed out the stereotypical and negative message which the image portrays. We can be aware too of the ready links which there can often be between Religious Education and the teaching about people and place as was outlined above in Chapter 1. The significance of the Good Samaritan was heightened as a member of an ethnic minority group, oppressed and despised (allegedly) by many of the Jews. He responded as the neighbour to the Jew travelling on the road to Jericho – no doubt a 'distant place' as far as they were both concerned.

The term 'distant' must also be used with care. Places which might be distant to some, are close – or certainly very familiar – to others. For some children in our schools, even the centre of town can be a 'distant place', as they rarely visit there. For some children living in country areas, even a first visit to a large city comes as a geography field trip when they reach secondary school. On the other hand, in a very real sense, Pakistan will be closer, and less distant for some children than another district in the city in which they are living.

## Building on personal geographies: clarifying values and maintaining balance in the curriculum

This brings us back to one of our starting points – the personal nature of children's geographical understanding. The ways in which children come to develop their knowledge about the world around them, and about people and place, are fundamentally shaped by their personal experience. The cultures of the household unit in which they are brought up, the physical and cultural landscape of their immediate environment, the pattern of their journeys on a daily, weekly or annual basis – all of these have a key determining influence on children's geographical understanding. It is no wonder therefore that a number of studies have shown how children's geographical knowledge and understanding is related to various social attributes, such as socioeconomic group, gender and ethnicity.

The primary teacher needs to recognise these facts and to develop their teaching on the basis of their knowledge of the children and their own cultural resources. There is a responsibility both to build upon existing knowledge and experience but also to extend that, so that each child is developing a steadily deepening and broadening understanding of the nature of the world in which they are living and on the significance of the relationships between people and the relationships between people and the physical world.

When working with children on people and place in the wider world, it is inevitable that there is a simplification of many of the features of a very complex world. One of the great problems or challenges facing the teacher is how to avoid trivialising the pictures we paint or the images children take away from the classroom. Similarly, the teacher will select certain characteristics or qualities of people and place for the learning activity with the children. What are the criteria which should determine the selection of these attributes? How do we ensure that the child is encouraged to see that there is always this danger of getting only part of the picture, or of getting too false or simplified a picture?

Geography is no more a neutral subject than politics. Although in Victorian times and well into this century it frequently posed as an objective and dispassionate enterprise which sought merely to describe ('capes and bays') and latterly to analyse ('locational analysis') the world, it is now widely accepted by geographers if not by all politicians that it is a heavily value-laden activity. From the choice of locations studied, through the methods used to study them, to the assumptions which are made in that study, there are values which influence the practice. These points are no less true of the study of geography by young children than they are of study at GCSE, A Level or in undergraduate and postgraduate programmes.

The debate around the creation of the National Curriculum for geography reflected the tension over this fact. The Secretary of State for Education at the time, Kenneth Clarke, sought to eradicate political issues from the document. Nevertheless, perhaps because of the growing strength of the green lobby in the electorate, the inclusion of environmental geography as an attainment target meant that politics and questions of values in geography could not be totally avoided. Some might argue that all geography is about the environment, therefore why separate it out? Nevertheless, as we have seen from the case studies above, the three-fold thematic distinction (physical, human, environmental) built into the National Curriculum may be quite a useful pedagogical device for enabling young learners to make sense of their world.

## National Curriculum primary geography and humanities – in the light of the 1995 revisions

The three classroom activities outlined above were identified before Sir Ron Dearing set out his draft proposals for a review of geography in the National Curriculum (May 1994). The children in all three groups greatly enjoyed their work, and gained much from it. The infants making maps, applying their personal geographical knowledge, the Year 6 juniors discussing earthquakes and volcanoes, and the Year 4 children investigating people and place in South Africa and beyond – these children had rich learning experiences which were obvious to all observers in their classrooms.

The consultation document for geography at Key Stage 2 recommended the teaching of:

(a) geographical skills – including reference to using maps;
(b) places – the school locality, plus two other locality studies;
(c) four themes: rivers, weather, settlements and environment.

At Key Stage 1 children are required to have opportunities to develop geographical skills, including using maps; to investigate two localities including that of the school; and to investigate the quality of the environment in a locality.

There is thus a strong emphasis upon locality scale studies. In the Key Stage 2 Programme of Study, the words 'place' and 'locality' appear frequently. The word 'map' is mentioned in at least seven distinct items. The word 'people' occurs but twice, although it is true there are occasional references to 'human activity', and to 'human processes'. Nevertheless it was interest in, and concern for, 'people' which sustained in large measure much of the interest for the 8–9-year-old children in Pilning. This interest in people ran alongside other elements of place, such as climate, deserts, wildlife, foods eaten, types of buildings.

Happily, by the time of writing, the situation in South Africa has changed dramatically since this classroom work took place (in the summer of 1993). Nevertheless, it was impressive how much the children derived from looking closely at people in the context of a place, and not simply at place, which might happen to include people as part of the locality. It is vital therefore that a strong focus upon **people** should underpin work in primary school geography within the National Curriculum. Among geographers an argument has raged over the extent to which geographical study should be concerned with people and social issues, or whether it should be more closely aligned to science. The latter position, with its emphasis on physical aspects of environment makes for a safer and less controversial area of study; it has the tacit support of many who do not really want children to question issues, particularly those with a political dimension. This tension between the various claims for geography is referred to by various writers, e.g. Knight (1993:39).

As a result of the Dearing review, primary children will still work with maps, but they will no longer study volcanoes as a statutory part of the National Curriculum. Perhaps primary teachers can teach some of the topics, like volcanoes, which fascinate children, in their 20% free time, the 'non-scheduled' National Curriculum time. There could be a temptation to concentrate upon core curriculum subjects, perhaps aiming for high results in national tests, and in school examination league tables where they are published. Taken together the three case studies show how geography as a subject and field of enquiry can be a vehicle for developing knowledge and cognitive skills across the curriculum. It also can be a tool for teachers aiming to promote humanitarian values among their children. As Wiegand (1993:1) writes 'Geography...has a potentially significant role in creating a better world.'

Finally it is worthwhile recalling an earlier consultation document – the Geography Working Party's interim report for the National Curriculum which included four key aims for teaching children geography in schools (DES, 1989a:6). In addition to developing knowledge about the 'earth's surface' and an 'informed concern about quality of the environment', a geographical education should:

b) foster a sense of wonder at the beauty of the world around them
d) ...enhance their sense of responsibility for the care of the earth and its peoples.

The learning activities of the 10–11-year-old children (volcanoes) and 8–9-year-old children (South Africa) were certainly enabling them to progress towards those aims. The 8–9 year olds were essentially involved in enhancing their 'sense of responsibility for the care of...(other) peoples'. All this took place alongside learning in other curriculum areas. What will happen to this kind of geography in post-Dearing primary classrooms?

# CHAPTER FOUR

## Stories, Values and the Challenges of Religious Education

## Introduction

For the purposes of this chapter, we have chosen to focus on the function of story and story-telling in religious education. In doing so we recognise that any successful pedagogy for religious education cannot and should not rely on this one medium (Watson, 1993:62) and that the use of artefacts and visits to places of worship, for example, are also essential processes. The central concerns of this chapter are the identification of appropriate aims for religious education, and the development of religious education programmes which include as many pupils as possible, including those who come from non-religious backgrounds. It is our view that the medium of story and the development and sharing of narratives, ranging from the fictional to the autobiographical, will provide at least a starting-point to the overarching questions of the book – what is special about human beings and how can teachers help to develop these special human qualities in children?

A feature of this chapter is a focus on the legal framework and statutory requirements for the teaching of religious education. The rationale for this is that religious education has been the subject of much debate and confusion, both before and after the 1989 Education Act. Since April 1993, documents about the teaching of religious education have been produced by the National Curriculum Council (1993a, b), Department for Education (DFE, 1994), Office for Standards in Education (OFSTED, 1994) and Schools Curriculum Assessment Authority (SCAA, 1994c). There are some inconsistencies between some of these recent documents and also between them and the specifications in the 1988 Education Act. We have chosen to include some discussion of these documents in the section of the chapter relating to the aims of religious education, because it is inappropriate to discuss these aims without some reference to the regulatory framework for religious education which is different from the arrangements for other National Curriculum subjects.

The presentation in this chapter seeks to find relationships between processes in religious education and the development of children's understanding of the effects of values and beliefs on human behaviour. We draw attention to the significance of these processes, in times of rapid change, to social activity within the school, within the local community and within the context of a new Europe and the wider world.

## The challenges of religious education

Religious education is a challenging subject to teach. It is difficult to define its aims and the content is controversial. A description of a short passage from a religious education lesson illustrates these points.

> A group of 8-year-old children are listening attentively to their teacher who is telling them the story of Noah's Ark. They have heard it many times before in assembly, during class topic work on 'water and colour' and in a musical production of Noah's Ark in which they had taken an active part 2 years earlier.
> At the end the teacher asks the question 'What was that story about?'
> A number of children respond to this question in concrete terms: 'it's about a flood', 'it's about a boat'. Other children indicate their developing powers of what some theorists would term abstract thinking, and declare that 'the story teaches us to look after the land', and 'it's about naughty children'.

It is hard to think what the right answer would be to this question, and it is in this respect that religious education is qualitatively different from some other curriculum subjects. For example, Benjamin Britten (the composer) and André Obey (the playwright), who both created celebrated works of art related to the theme of the Great Flood, would have been able to answer this question, but their answers would have been substantially different from each other, and probably different again from answers given by the Chief Rabbi or a feminist theologian such as Mary Daly. Yet all of these answers would have come from informed and educated people. Their answers would have ranged from the factual to the imaginative to the spiritual and it would perhaps be unhelpful to try to decide whose answer was best or whether our own answers would have been any more satisfactory.

Other related problems emerge which pose great challenges to teachers. For example, teachers may have a commitment to a particular faith or an equally strong commitment to having no faith at all. Others may be concerned about aspects of indoctrination or even hypocrisy when dealing with children who will come from a wide variety of religious or non-religious backgrounds. There is scope for so many misunderstandings.

A purpose of this chapter is to discuss such problems and in so doing we will emphasise how different genres of stories and writing can be used in the classroom to support children's learning in religious education. We will offer a framework for planning work with children and we will provide some case study material to illustrate these more theoretical aspects. The chapter has been written both for the non-specialist primary teacher and for those who work closely with such teachers. Its purpose is to provide some ideas for starting-points and to outline some basic processes to shape and direct the work undertaken.

## The structuring of religious education after the 1988 Education Reform Act

A first confusion arises because the legal framework regulating religious education has been subject to some recent changes. Since 1988 religious education has been included in the basic curriculum for all registered pupils aged 4–19. This was consistent with the requirements of the 1944 Education Act. However, the Education Reform Act of 1988 set religious education within the context of the spiritual, moral, cultural, mental and physical development of pupils and of society. These dimensions now underpin the curriculum and their importance is reinforced by their place in the new inspection framework for schools following the 1992 Education Act. This Act requires the inspectorate to keep the Secretary of State informed about the spiritual, moral, social and cultural development of pupils.

It is perhaps surprising that when plans were being made to nationalise all of the other curriculum subjects, a decision was made that religious education should continue to be determined on a local basis. The rationale for the local determination of religious education programmes was that the religious make-up of each local area is distinctive and particular, and that the curricula for religious education should reflect these local differences. The details of the regulatory framework are set out in DES Circular 3/89 which was issued in January 1989 (DES, 1989d). A principal requirement of this circular is that it is the responsibility of Standing Advisory Councils on Religious Education (SACREs) to develop locally agreed syllabuses for religious education.

The general role of the SACRE is:

> to advise the authority upon such matters connected with religious worship in county schools and the religious education to be given in accordance with an agreed syllabus as the authority may refer to the council or as the council may see fit. (DES, 1989d)

The functions of SACREs have been slightly changed as a result of the Education Act 1993, and these changes are summarised in DFE Circular 1/94 issued in January 1994 (DFE, 1994). A new requirement is that the Local Education Authorities (LEAs) must convene an 'agreed syllabus conference' to review the Agreed Syllabus every 5 years.

The new legislation has preserved the rights of parents to withdraw their children from religious education and collective worship. Teachers continue to have the right to withdraw themselves. The new legislation has reinforced the provision of the 1944 Education Act that religious education must not seek to convert pupils or to seek to impose on them any particular religion or denomination. This ruling does not apply to grant aided and special agreement schools.

In January 1994, as the result of a government initiative 'to look into the teaching of RE and rescue it from the poor status it too often holds and to raise standards' (SCAA, 1994c), the SCAA produced a framework for two model syllabuses. The document is not binding and is intended to constitute advice to agreed syllabus conferences. SCAA has been careful to involve wide-ranging representation of six of the religions present in the country – Buddhism, Christianity, Hinduism, Islam, Judaism, and Sikhism.

In January 1994 the Dearing Report indicated that the time spent on religious education should be 36 hours per year in Key Stage 1 and 45 hours per year in Key Stage 2, equivalent to the time spent on other foundation subjects (SCAA, 1994b).

A new legal requirement in the 1988 Act has brought about changes, through its requirement that an Agreed Syllabus should 'reflect the fact that the religious traditions of Great Britain are in the main Christian while taking account of the other principal religions represented in Great Britain' (DES, 1989d). The wording of this legally binding clause has been subject to much debate and discussion. This legal requirement, which is binding on all syllabuses devised by SACREs after 1989, was expected to have the positive effect of broadening the content of syllabuses in many LEAs.

It is not only in recent years that religious education has been the subject of change, and it is interesting that such changes often reflect shifts in the cultural, social, economic and political spheres. Hull has presented an interesting analysis of such changes over the last 120 years. He has identified distinct theological phases in central government's activity (Hull, 1993). Thus the 'neutral' approach of studying the Bible through the history and geography of Palestine was seen to be appropriately bland in the 1870s, in a period when the issue of the struggle between denominations was seen to be potentially divisive in the education sphere:

> Whether this could be called the teaching of Christianity is a moot point, but it is enough to note that the fear of plurality found expression in a religious education which sought refuge in the neutrality of antiquity. (Hull, 1993)

He argues that following the rise of the ecumenical movement and the diminution of denominational rivalry, a second phase was characterised by a concern to identify and promote those Christian values which might be a counter to the forces of communism and fascism which were becoming more apparent from the mid-1920s. He characterises the third theological phase as the dialogical, a phase which reaches from the 1960s to the 1980s, a period in which there was an emphasis in religious education 'upon dialogue between the pupils and religion and a dialogue between the religions themselves as a stimulus to the quest for orientation and meaning in life' (Hull, 1993). The Swann Report *Education for All* (DES, 1985) in part reflects this phase, through its promotion of a religious education programme which would draw upon all the spiritual traditions of the country.

In the 1980s the struggle between competing ideologies became more evident to the public when there was wide newspaper coverage of the tensions between the approach of the 'multiculturalists', as typified by the recommendations of the Swann Report to the Department of Education and Science, and a new thrust by the traditionalists and free marketeers of the 'new right', as typified in the writings of the Hillgate Group (Hillgate Group, 1986). Baroness Cox, herself a member of this group, argued in the House of Lords that Christianity was part of British heritage, that multi-faith approaches were eroding the integrity of the Christian faith and of other faiths and that parents were being denied the reassurance that their children would receive a Christian-based education in schools in Britain (Hansard, 1988).

Although the wording of the legislation (cited above) of the 1988 Education Reform Act reflected some kind of resolution between these conflicting ideologies, the issue continues to be contested. This wording remains, although a recent circular from the DFE (DFE, 1994) which describes Christianity as the 'predominant' religion (a new descriptor) has again reminded teachers and other educators that the compromise is an uneasy one.

There is of course a danger in assuming that political rhetoric reflects what is actually happening in schools. The conclusion of a recent report by OFSTED (1994) on *Religious Education and Collective Worship 1992–1993* would seem to suggest that the multiculturalists, anti-racists and proponents of multifaith approaches have in fact had little impact on the content of the primary curriculum for religious education:

> despite the declared objectives of many school policies and agreed
> syllabuses, and contrary to the widespread public perception that current RE
> teaching has abandoned Christianity, many pupils are not taught about world
> religions other than Christianity.

This is an important finding and teachers now need to consider whether such a narrow focus is appropriate for a preparation for life in the 1990s and beyond. Such an emphasis on Christianity would do little to meet the needs either of children from different religious backgrounds or of those from non-religious backgrounds. It would not address the wider societal issues of xenophobia and intolerance which are readily discernible in Britain and in the wider European context.

The complexity of the processes of religious education requires a clear formulation of general aims. Thus we have tried to identify a concise set of basic aims to underpin the kind of approach described in this chapter.

## Establishing aims for religious education

The premise of the discussions in this chapter is that religious education should aim to:

(a) Give pupils an understanding of what it means to take a religion seriously – this involves the promotion of knowledge and understanding so as to safeguard the freedoms and rights of different religious groups within a democracy. This is a fundamental aim of any religious education in a plural society which seeks to protect itself against the dangers of intolerance and racism. It is consistent with and supportive of the Council of Europe recommendation of the Committee of Ministers to member states on the teaching and learning about human rights in schools (*see* Starkey, 1991:256).

(b) Promote an awareness of the full potential of the human being – this involves the provision of opportunities for pupils to explore and share those experiences which are special to human beings and should include:

- the recognition of the spiritual development of individual children;
- the development of an awareness of an overarching human response to questions of morality and of a sensitivity to moral dilemmas;
- the development of a pupil's confidence in her or his own cultural identity.

(c) Develop an understanding of the influence of different religious traditions on the lives of individuals and communities – this involves a study of the teachings of different religious traditions and of the values and visions afforded through these traditions. This strand can provide opportunities for pupils to review and strengthen their own life stances for themselves. In this sense it is an essential component of any religious education, in that it provides substance for the spiritual, moral and cultural development of pupils at school and of society, as required by Section 1 of the Education Reform Act 1988.

These aims are interrelated and of course they are not new. Indeed versions of them can be identified in writings about religious education from the 1970s (for example Holm, 1976), through such curriculum development projects as the FARE Project (Copley and Priestly, 1991) and in recent publications coming from Westhill College (Read *et al* ,. 1992). The aims as identified here relate closely to headings found in the SCAA document *Model Syllabuses for Religious Education* (SCAA, 1994c), which are:

- Learning about religion,
- Learning about human experience,
- Learning from human experience,
- Learning from religion.

What is important is that teachers recognise the connections between these processes in planning and in delivery. The interdependence of the processes is indicated in Figure 4.1. This attempts to illustrate the relationship between the curriculum (or RE programme), the worlds of the children and the wider society of which we are all a part. The inner circle represents the programme as it is experienced by the children. The arrows represent points of access, influences and outcomes.

The effects of a religious education programme can be discerned in the direction of the arrows which emphasise the following points:

(a) Access to the programme may depend on the inclusion of discussion of the children's own experience. There will be many children in our schools who do not have first-hand experience of religion and the entry point for this diverse group can be facilitated through discussion and exploration of experiences which everybody shares.

(b) The output of the programme derives from what is shared and learnt 'about and from human experience' as well as 'about and from religion'. The

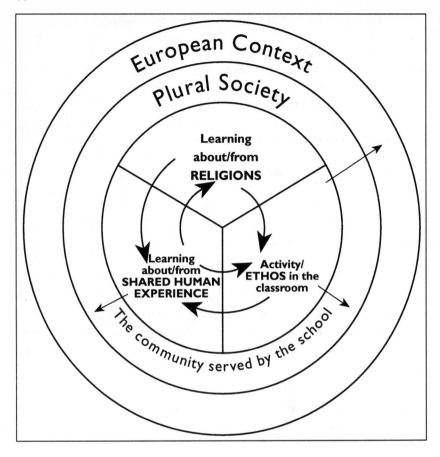

**Figure 4.1** Processes in teaching religious education

hope is that successful learning will have an effect on the quality of the learning environment. This would be discernible through the openness and tolerance of the pupils in their interactions with each other. The teacher will be able to support the children and make connections between their learning in religious education and their learning in other curriculum areas.

(c) Successful learning will also affect the pupils' views of and outlook on the plural society of which they themselves are a part and which is itself a part of a new and developing European community.

What are the practical implications of such an approach? In the sections which follow, the discussion will centre around the medium of story-telling as a vehicle for learning. This is arranged around two headings: 'The role of story in learning about and from religion' and 'The role of story in learning about and from human experience'.

# The role of story in learning about and from religion

A extract from the SCAA document (1994c) provides a useful example of how story can support learning about and from religion. The extract is drawn from the 'Model 1' syllabus and details some possible approaches to teaching about Buddhism in Key Stage 1. The guidelines suggest that a learning programme should include specific 'Knowledge and Understanding' about aspects which are important to Buddhists:

- stories about the life of the Buddha;
- the moral teachings of the Buddha;
- the Buddhist community;

The guidelines also some examples of 'Learning experiences' for the children. A close examination of one section of these guidelines, the moral teaching of the Buddha, illustrates how the pupils could be involved in learning about Buddhism, learning about and from their shared human experience and learning from the Buddhist tradition.

- *Knowledge and understanding*: Moral teaching of the Buddha
  - People should be kind and compassionate, generous, truthful and patient.
  - They should not hurt any living thing, steal or tell lies.

- Learning experiences (these are examples only):
  - Talk about how people show kindness to each other.
  - Think about when we hurt people or animals, steal and tell lies and why people believe these things are wrong.
  - Identify other things they believe are wrong.

There is an equivalent section for pupils in Key Stage 2 which, as can be expected, contains more detailed information (for example, about the Four Noble Truths) and requires more complex discussion (for example, about how selfishness and greed might cause suffering).

These examples from the model programmes of study involve learning outcomes related to learning *about* religion – acquiring and developing knowledge and understanding of a particular religion (Buddhism) and developing awareness of the influence of this religion. They also promote learning outcomes related to learning *from* religion – encountering religious and moral issues, enhancing pupils' own spiritual and moral development and developing positive attitudes towards other people and their right to hold different beliefs. The decision about the organisation and ordering of the teaching programme is left to the teacher, who may decide to start with providing information about the Buddha and Buddhism, or who may decide that the pupils' involvement will be maximised if their own experience is the first subject of discussion.

A teacher who decides to start with the experiences of the children may easily turn to a picture/story-book which is relevant to these themes (for example, how people show kindness to each other) and which is relevant to the lives of the children in the class. *Dogger*, by Shirley Hughes (1978), is a well-known story that could be used to explore the theme of acts of kindness.

Davey in *Dogger* loses his much-loved toy dog; the house is ransacked from top to bottom but the dog is not found, and Davey is distraught. On the day of the school jumble sale Dogger reappears as an item for sale. Davey desperately rushes through the crowd to get the money from his parents only to return to find his treasure has been bought by another child. The day is saved by an act of kindness from Davey's older sister Bella.

In a follow-up to such a story, children could begin to discuss acts of kindness which they had experienced in their own lives; a discussion which could, if appropriate, lead to a discussion of the moral teachings of the Buddha.

Within religious education stories have been described as 'the common coin of religious experience without which most religious ideas would not touch the hearts of ordinary people' (Wiltshire County Council, 1987). Many great religious educators of the world have used story, and stories are commonly used in schools by teachers who draw on the full range of myths, legends, biographies, autobiographies and fictions. By selecting from these forms and by using them in the classroom even primary school teachers who are at their most diffident when approaching religious education can fulfil the basic aims identified earlier in this chapter. This is a strategy which is emphasised through Agreed Syllabuses for LEAs across England and Wales. For example, the Agreed Syllabus for the County of Avon indicates that at Key Stage 1 children should have the opportunity to:

- explore many different aspects of experience through a wide variety of stories, including religious stories (e.g. stories about Jesus, stories that Jesus told, Old Testament stories, Muslim tales of Nasruddin, Hindu myths);
- reflect upon the books and stories which are special to them and consider the reasons why they mean so much;
- begin to perceive that some stories, including religious stories, have a 'hidden message' (e.g. Aesop's fables, the parables of Jesus).

This extract provides examples of how teachers are encouraged to use story to provide opportunities for learning about religion as well as for learning from and through shared human experience.

Not all religions have a developed theology but all have collections of stories which are central to their beliefs. Stories from different religious traditions, stories found in the Bible, the Ramayana or those of the life of the Buddha have all been carefully constructed and patterned so that their use can enable pupils to become acquainted with a religious community and deepen their knowledge of their own traditions as well as those of others. These stories were conceived and constructed as 'educational', illuminating aspects of the religious faith that doctrine could not define.

Biographical material has an important role in illustrating the significance of religion to the lives of people who are well known and whose actions have been celebrated, for example Ann Frank, the Pilgrim Fathers, Mother Theresa, Martin Luther King, Desmond Tutu, Ghandi or Friedl Dicker-Brandejs. Such stories can provide links with other curriculum areas.

## The role of story in learning about and from shared human experience

Stories can be used to help young children understand the effects of values and beliefs on human behaviour, including their own. They can help children gain experience of a range of emotions and to explore and evaluate human responses to difficult situations within the relatively secure environment of the classroom. Teachers will know many stories themselves which have moved and affected the children they teach. Two such stories about human activity on and around the American continent are described below.

*Story one:* The picture/story-book *Going West* (Wadell and Dupasquier, 1983). The authors tell the story through the eyes of the young writer Kate (a diary writer) of a journey by waggon-train by a group of early settlers in North America. We learn of her family's adventures sharing her feelings of excitement, fear, hope and ambivalence. An older sister Louisa becomes ill and dies of typhoid. With simple effect the writers draw us in to Kate's struggle to make meaning from her sister's death and burial:

> We had to leave Louisa behind. Mr Ridger says God will look after Louisa because she was so small. Louisa was bigger than me.

Further themes that are explored are encounters with native Americans and the acquisition of their land, and the rebuilding of a family group following a period of intense struggle.

*Story 2:* Another picture story-book describing a recent event that was televised across the northern hemisphere – *The Story of Three Whales* by G. Whittell (1988). Three whales are trapped in the ice at the start of winter off the north coast of Alaska. The local population gets to know them well and many people visit the hole in the ice at which they gather. They become concerned for their safety as the rest of the whale population has already migrated. The youngest whale disappears without trace. Television viewers are updated on the story day by day and an ice-breaking ship from Russia tries to rescue them without success. They eventually head off under the ice but nobody knows their fate. Did they ever make it to the open sea?

These stories can touch deep thoughts and feelings and can evoke a sense of mystery. The point has already been made in this chapter that for a religious education programme to be appropriate for all pupils, including those who come from non-religious backgrounds, there need to be opportunities to discuss and explore such significant aspects of human experience which are common to all. Read *et al.* (1992) have identified a helpful list of themes designed to draw out those aspects of human experience which are significant to religious education. These include the themes of 'The Natural World', 'Relationships', 'Rules and Issues', 'Stages of Life', 'Celebrations', 'Lifestyles', and 'Suffering'. All of these are explored in the two stories which have been described. They are also themes which are common to many of the locally agreed syllabuses.

The stories described are distinctive because they are complex and multi-layered. In another genre of story, the folk-tale and fairy-story, the polarisation of good and evil, hatred and love can help some young children who are more responsive to literal meanings to develop insights into themselves, their relationships and their own actions and behaviours. This particular genre can also be enjoyed at a multiplicity of levels.

*Story 3: The story of King Jahangir and the Baby.* This story comes from the excellent Storytellers' Series published by Andre Deutsch (1988). These stories originate from the oral traditions of many different countries and were collected by the members (parents, teachers and children) of the Reading Materials for Minority Groups Project in the London Boroughs of Haringey and Barnet. This story begins: 'One day two women came to the palace and rang the bell. They were fighting about a baby.'

Nursery children being read this story were shocked when the wise king suggested cutting the baby in half:

– He's not a cake.
– That would hurt him.
– He didn't want to be cut up.

They were reassured when the baby was saved:

- His mummy would not want him hurt.
- He's happy now.

The challenge for the story-teller, and of course for the teacher, is to use strategies that stimulate interest in and reflection on the human issues that emerge. A range of ideas for promoting interest in and awareness of stories are presented in recent publications by Hammond and Hay (1990) and by Lamont and Burns (1993). A simple technique familiar to children and adults alike is the 'interrupted story' – the presentation of an unfinished story which invites the interest of the listeners or audience and their collaborative participation in resolving the issues and dilemmas faced by the characters.

The readiness for young children to involve themselves in such collaborative fiction writing can be illustrated by a case study.

A class of 7- and 8-year-old children in an urban school were facing some interpersonal difficulties during their first weeks in a new school – the 'Junior School' – which was on a different site from their previous 'Infant School' and which had different and unfamiliar facilities in the school playground. The supervising staff had been overwhelmed by the need to help children resolve disputes of the kind which are familiar to primary-school staff across the UK. The teacher decided to include an element of curriculum work related to 'human relationships' in the programme for the class. An example of a resource for learning used by the teacher was part of a poster, produced by the Quaker Society of Friends, which depicts a dilemma facing two donkeys who are unsure of how to resolve a particular conflict of interest (Figure 4.2).

The task for the children was to work in small groups (twos and threes) to discuss possible solutions to this problem and to draw a picture to depict a possible end of the story. The children were able to engage in this activity with ease and examples of their solutions are presented below (Figures 4.3–4.6).

In a subsequent session in the same day, the teacher presented all of the drawings to the class using the overhead projector. She invited the children to discuss which 'solutions' were most fair and which were most unfair and to consider whether human beings (including themselves) ever had problems like this. The ensuing discussion showed that children were able to apply the concept of fairness not only to the story of the donkeys but also to other real-life situations which they described. These situations included experiences at home (disputes between family members), at school (disputes within

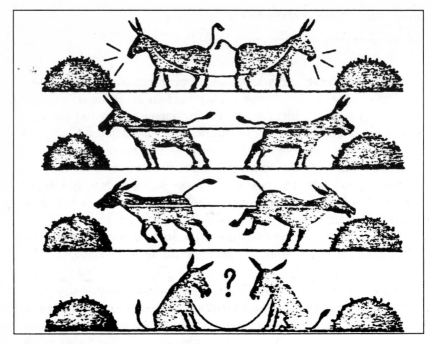

**Figure 4.2** The donkeys' problem

the classroom and playground) and in the wider world (issues which they had begun to learn about from television news items).

There are opportunities within this kind of activity to make explicit reference to the teachings of different religious communities about human relationships. Watson (1993) identifies relevant extracts from six different religious texts.

*Sikhism:* 'As thou deemest thyself, so deem others.' (Kabir)

**Figure 4.3** The donkeys' problem – a child's solution

One donkey sits down and eats and the other stands up.

**Figure 4.4** The donkeys' problem – a child's solution

The donkeys are trying to cut the rope with their teeth and their tails.

**Figure 4.5** The donkeys' problem – a child's solution

**Figure 4.6** The donkeys' problem – a child's solution

| *Judaism:* | 'What is hateful to you, do not do to your fellow man.' (Talmud: Shabbat 31a) |
| *Islam:* | 'No one of you is a believer until he loves for his brother what he loves for himself.' (Forty Hadith of an-Nawawi 13) |
| *Hinduism:* | 'Do not to others what if done to you would cause you pain.' (Mahabharata, Anusasana Parva 113.8) |
| *Christianity:* | 'Always treat others as you would like them to treat you.' (Matthew: 7:12) |
| *Buddhism:* | 'Hurt not others with that which pains yourself.' (Samyutta Nikaya V.353) |

Such sacred writings could be used to demonstrate to children that, for religious communities, rules about morality develop from their understanding of God or of Nature, but that such codes are in many ways consistent with human rights principles. It may be reassuring for children to learn about a commonality of response from diverse religious communities to the question of how human beings should behave, and to recognise that justice is a common aspiration for human beings, whether or not they are from religious backgrounds.

The discussion of the different possible resolutions to the 'Donkeys' Problem' indicated that children were able to apply a concept when evaluating behaviours – in this case the concept of 'fairness'. This will not be news to any who have worked with young children and who know how quick they are to address the question of justice and fairness within their own social setting.

The facility to understand the meaning of allegories (for example the Donkeys' Problem) and analogies is particularly pertinent to children's reading of stories related to religious education. A colleague in school has recently written an account which describes how children can become confused if this technique is not understood:

> For example, the story of the houses built on sand and rock. This story was told as part of a topic on "Houses and Homes". The teacher told the story and asked the children "Which foundation was better?". "The rock" replied the children. 'Yes, here we have a story that teaches us that houses built on strong foundations will stand despite the storms'.
>
> If this was a lesson on Design Technology then the point was very valid and instructive. However, as an RE lesson there has been no religious truth/ meaning brought out at all. As far as the children were concerned "Jesus would tell you to build houses on rock if you want them to last!". However, the story is a parable; there is a hidden meaning to be found. The story has significance for the lives of the children, a very useful tool for their future decision-making processes. It is a story which needs to be put into its context. Jesus is not talking about houses but about lives built on strong convictions. What other underlying points have the children taken away with them? Possibly "Jesus is a housebuilder!". How then having learnt about the houses, how would they interpret Jesus saying "I shall tear down the Temple after 3 days". Maybe they would think "Jesus has moved into the demolition business now!".' (Mlewa, 1994)

Even where the meaning of a story is clear, we still need to question what actual learning has taken place, and whether such learning would constitute the development of a moral sense:

> Some 6–8-year-old children who had been learning about the parable of the 'Good Samaritan' were questioned by their teacher about what they thought the point of the lesson had been. The replies came quite slowly, but included:
>> 'It taught us about how people used to live in the olden days.'
>> 'It was about the clothes they wore then.'
>> 'We looked at a map.'
> It was only late in the discussion that someone suggested that the story was 'about how to look after other people'. At this point a most revealing remark was made by another child:
>> 'A story doesn't make any difference. You still do the same things afterwards anyway.'

This is a response of which we have to be mindful as teachers but surely one which we will need to continue to challenge through our practice. A major challenge is to find contexts to which the children can relate (and maybe the road to Jericho is too distant in place and time) and to find voices which allow children to make those essential connections between values, beliefs and behaviours. Certainly we should never underestimate the power of the voices of other children to communicate experiences and understandings. The power of peer group learning, especially in the social sphere, is widely recognised in primary schools. Many teachers have been able to draw on children's own narratives in making links between values, beliefs and behaviours. These often relate to environmental themes, to personal experiences of religious festivals and to social issues arising in the school context and in the wider world. Such narratives are often presented within the frame of a school assembly and provide opportunities for a sharing of principles to underpin the ethos of the school community.

A new and moving collection of children's voices, many of them of primary-school age, has been published by the Zidovske Muzeum in Prague (Zidovske Muzeum, 1993). These children were living with their parents in Terezin in Bohemia between 1941 and 1944 when the town functioned as a ghetto town to which Jewish families were moved prior to their deportation to the extermination camps in Nazi-occupied territories to the East. The collection features self-expression by the children through poetry and the visual arts. The quality of the drawings and paintings can in part be attributed to the teaching of the artist Friedl Dicker-Brandejs, who lived in the L410 home for girls in Terezin. The writings contain deeply sensitive responses to the reality of human conditions in the Terezin ghetto. Some examples of these writings may serve as reminder of the power of children's own expressions to make sense of experience and make connections with other human beings across time and place.

**The Garden**
A little garden,
Fragrant and full of roses.
The path is narrow
And a little boy walks along it.
A little boy, a sweet boy,
Like that growing blossom.
When the blossom comes to bloom,
The little boy will be no more.
Franta Bass, 4.9.1930 – 28.10.1944

**Yes, that's the way things are**
In Terezin in the so-called park

An old granddad sits
Somewhere there in the so-called park.
He wears a beard down to his lap
and on his head, a little cap
Hard crusts he crumbles in his gums,
He's only got one single tooth.
My poor old man with working gums,
Instead of soft rolls, lentil soup.
My poor old grey beard!

Miroslav Kosek, 30.3.1932 – 19.10.1944
Hanus Lowy Bachner, 29.6.1931 – 4.10.1944

**It all depends on how you look at it**
Terezin is full of beauty.
It's in your eyes now clear
And through the street the tramp
Of many marching feet I hear.

In the ghetto at Terezin,
It looks that way to me
Is a square kilometre of earth
Cut off from the world that's free.
Death, after all, claims everyone

You find it everywhere.
It catches up with even those
Who wear their noses in the air.

The whole, wide world is ruled
With a certain justice, so
That helps perhaps to sweeten
The poor man's pain and woe.

Miroslav Kosek, 30.3.1932 – 19.10.1944

**I am a Jew**
I am a Jew, a Jew I shall remain,
Even if I die of hunger
I will not give up my nation,
I will fight always
For my nation, on my honour.
I will never be ashamed
of my nation, on my honour.
I am proud of my nation,
A nation most worthy of honour.
I shall always be oppressed,
I shall always live again.

Franta Bass, 4.9.1930 – 28.10.1944

At the time that two of us purchased these texts in Prague (September 1994), we noted that the security of the celebration of the Jewish new year at the Pinkas Synagogue depended on the presence of armed military guards. We have also read recently of the publication of research findings of the Bristol based organisation SARI (Stance Against Racist Incidents) which indicate that the numbers of racist attacks have increased significantly in the Bristol area – a phenomenon which inevitably affects the everyday lives of (among others) those Muslim and Hindu communities who inhabit the city. The need for religious education to inform pupils about their own society and about the different communities within it is as pressing as ever. So is the need to use stories and create narratives with children which promote a confidence in their own developing life stances and which reflect a commitment to social justice and a respect for others.

# CHAPTER FIVE

# *Environmental Education*

Study of history, geography and religious education has a particularly important part to play in helping pupils to clarify their values towards the environment. (National Curriculum Council, 1990b)

In the preceding chapters we have concentrated on three 'subjects' – history, geography and religious education – in raising questions about the nature of humanities in the primary curriculum, and about how children have knowledge and experience of these areas.

We continue this examination of the role of humanities in the primary curriculum, taking some cross-curricular themes to provide a vehicle for this. This chapter, which focuses on environmental education, is followed by chapters on education for citizenship and 'European dimensions'.

In this chapter we think about how children respond to 'the environment' and what it means to them. We also explore some of the ways in which 'the environment' might feature as a curriculum element. This exploration in turn raises questions about the values and attitudes that all adults have about environmentalism and about environmental education.

In the first part of the chapter, the work of an infant teacher with 6–7-year-old children is described. She experiments by using part of the school environment to provide a forum for enquiry, observation, and enjoyment. The children's responses illustrate environmental education as a way of 'learning in, through and about the environment'.

Questions about the place of environmental education in helping children 'learn to care for the environment', including the development of school conservation areas, are then raised. We give an account of the work of Jeff Hague who has been active for many years, helping children learn to 'care for the environment'. This work enables us to introduce other potentially worthwhile outcomes of environmental education. These include:

- helping children with special educational needs;
- activity-based learning; differentiating for different abilities;
- building self-esteem in children who lack confidence;
- developing a supportive school ethos;
- encouraging parental involvement in schools;
- children developing cross-curricular considerations.

In the last part of the chapter some different emphases in environmental education are presented. We consider where we would set the parameters of environmental education, and the nature of the questions with which teachers and children might profitably engage in the classroom. The social dimension of environmental education is considered in relation to the work of 9–11 year olds working with the topic of 'the homeless'. The questions raised here are about the kind of responsibility and the degree of involvement we accept for other people in the community, both local and global. This also leads us to question the traditional role of natural science as the curriculum slot where environmental enquiry takes place. We argue that it should be humanities, rather than science, that is at the core of the schools' curriculum.

## Environmental education: learning in through and about the environment

'Environmental education' has existed in various forms for a long time, although it has been much more visible in recent years, with the growing awareness of threats to the environment. We can easily see, for example, how 'global warming' and the disappearance of the equatorial rain forests have become widely canvassed issues.

It is also worthy of note that the inclusion of environmental education (of some sort) within a broad and balanced National Curriculum has the support of people from across the political and ideological spectrum. We have already seen how within National Curriculum geography, environmental geography is given a prominent position, involving pupils in the study of controversial issues, despite the fact that the former Secretary of State for Education, Kenneth Clarke, was keen to reduce the provision for possible controversial issues (in both the geography curriculum and the history curriculum, *see* Graham, 1993).

From birth, babies are developing their environmental awareness. Through touch, sight and sound, they are active explorers of the world around them. For such young children the presence of other people, above all their parents, is the most important element within the environment.

There is a danger that for older children and adults, the roles and needs of others in the community are underplayed when thinking in terms of 'the environment':

**Figure 5.1** Children learning from the environment

Paula Knee is a teacher of infant children in Coniston Infants School, Bristol. She decided as a new venture to take her 6–7-year-old children on an environmental trail. This was a walk lasting about an hour and a half. It led from school, through a housing area with shops, to undeveloped grounds used by older children for riding their bikes, to a recently developed business park. The children's observations and activities were structured by guidelines produced for adult volunteers (mainly parents) who accompanied her with the children.

This being the first time Paula had tried an activity of this kind, she was keen to see how valuable it would be in trying to assess children's learning in geographical knowledge and skills. She was also interested in the response of the children to this new kind of activity.

There were 13 children in the party, and Paula with her adult helpers. The children took part in different activities at stages on the walk such as listening, sketching, making rubbings, observing, simple written recording, and using a map (Figure 5.1). Skills will be apparent here. She also sought to assess and record in a variety of ways what the children had learned and what they felt they had learned from this environmental trail.

Paula's children enjoyed themselves in many ways on their environmental trail. These are some of the statements they made when asked afterwards to talk about their walk:

'We had to collect leaves. We had a piece of paper that we put a line on when we saw a car. I did four lines. We had a piece of paper and a crayon, we had to put it on the floor and rub it in. That was my favourite.' *(Nikki)*

'There was a duck on the pond that couldn't fly. I liked the ducks. One came and stood by me then I went back to Coniston Infants by the gate for a short cut. Mrs D, Miss K and Cathy's Mum went with us.' *(Rhianna)*

'I liked splashing in the mud puddles. When we were getting near the school we ran over the hill. I saw lots of swans and ducks. Me and Robbie were walking in the mud. We had a fun day.' *(Sasha)*

These were views of the children on an excursion planned by their class teacher to promote their awareness of and curiosity about the environment. She had also sought to stimulate 'learning in, through and about the environment'. These children's remarks are part of the evidence that this had been a stimulating experience. Paula recognised from these and other responses they had deepened their knowledge and awareness of people and the world immediately around them, as they explored the built environment around their homes.

Typically, and understandably, some of the events which stayed uppermost in their minds were different from the intended aspects of knowledge, understanding, skills, and values identified in advance by their teacher. Nevertheless, while enjoying themselves with their friends, they had engaged with some of the more formal aspects of learning as identified within the National Curriculum such as using maps, elements of maths, and recording skills. No doubt for some the development of English and communication skills had particular benefits. Paula Knee evaluated this environmental trail as a very successful learning activity for her children, and a useful way of assessing children's learning in geography. She hoped to share these outcomes with other colleagues so that this environmental work could be part of ongoing curriculum activities within the school.

## The development of environmental education in the primary curriculum

In engaging her children in this way, Paula was enacting some of the suggestions for effective learning advocated in the Plowden Report (DES, 1967). The report extols the value of making 'Use of the Environment' (p.199) as an 'effective way of integrating the curriculum' by drawing upon the 'boundless curiosity which children have about the world about them.' In this two-page section on 'Use of the Environment', the report emphasises to the physical attributes of the school environment, without much reference to values or issues. The Plowden Report has been criticised (Bantock, 1969; Dearden, 1976) for the supposed overemphasis upon children's 'learning by discovery' without sufficient structure or teacher guidance. The half-page discussion of 'discovery learning', following the environment section, clearly sets out the role of the teacher in 'discovery learning': '(the) teacher is responsible for encouraging children in enquiries which lead to discovery and for asking leading questions'. This is very different to the picture of directionless classroom activities painted by some critics of 'progressive' education.

Environmental education has been a relatively uncontentious area of the curriculum in both primary and secondary schools for 30 or more years now. Its roots can be traced back even before Plowden certainly to the first half of the century. The Hadow Report of 1931 commended visits to local places to support learning in 'history, geography and nature study' (Hadow Committee, 1931).

Environmental education has not featured prominently in every primary school but it has been a conspicuous curriculum component in many. In such schools since the early 1970s there has been a steady refinement in form and coherence, moving on from vaguely defined local studies or rural studies.

In 1968 the Blandford *Approaches to Environmental Studies* were published. These were revised and enlarged 3 years later (Perry, Jones and Hammersley, 1971). The general educational approach of the Handbook and related texts reflected Plowden's view of 'learning by discovery'. The authors set out their basic philosophy in introducing the series. Active learning by way of enquiry and investigation was encouraged. Cross-curricular approaches were promoted to overcome the limitations of what was seen as too rigid a subject differentiated curriculum in primary classrooms. An integrated approach to learning was advocated to offset the constraints, and sometimes the irrelevance, of subject domination:

> The content of our schools' curricula developed largely from the few traditional subjects which were regarded as essential for a child...(but) added extra subjects until timetables became overloaded. At certain fixed intervals during the school day there was a change from one subject to another, often with no sign of relevance, and this pattern was followed day after day and year after year. (Perry *et al.*, 1971:12)

The series of texts published in this Blandford environmental collection were valuable resources to support topic work in school. Emphasis was placed upon learning about visual aspects of the environment – roads, villages, churches. Children were encouraged to investigate, enquiry skills were developed, and a stimulus was provided for field-work.

Another stimulus for environmental education in the 1970s was The Schools Council series *Project Environment* (Colton and Morgan, 1974). This acknowledged the impetus given by the United Nations 1972 Conference on the Human Environment. The philosophy of The Schools Council included the need to 're-educate society to its responsibility' and echoed parts of the United States Environmental Education Act 1970. Some of the topics included population, resource use and recycling, water, pollution, environmental quality, and man in nature (sic).

In encouraging children to develop a sense of our joint responsibility to guard against threats to the environment, the importance of avoiding indoctrination was stressed, as was ensuring children understood the issues involved. This approach involved seeing how we are all 'directly or indirectly responsible for problems, and all have a positive part to play in meeting them' (Colton and Morgan, 1974:7).

Other writers such as Pamela Mays (1985), highlighted the teaching of subjects by learning through the environment. She argued that explorations in the environment would enable children to deepen their knowledge in specified subject areas.

Many of these books promoted 'learning in, through, and about the environment'; while less emphasis was given to 'learning for' the environment. This aspect was more evident in The Schools Council Project Environment and in popular works by authors such as Colin Ward and Anthony Fyson e.g. *Streetwork: The Exploding school* (Ward and Fyson, 1973). Sometimes local environment investigations were linked with personal and oral history; for example *St. Paul's People Talking to Children from St. Barnabas School* (Bristol Broadsides, 1983).

In primary schools in the 1970s and 1980s it was not uncommon for 'environmental studies' to be the term used to cover history and geography, and this curriculum area was frequently linked with topic work. During the 1980s a more active approach to environmental education, emphasising the concepts of care and conservation, was encouraged through the development in many schools of conservation areas. Some schools worked on brightening up their grounds; others set out to provide children with first-hand experience of natural phenomena – flowers, minibeasts, and pond life. In some, like the Park School, Kingswood, children were actively involved in planning and designing improvements in the school grounds. This work was linked with Economic and Industrial Understanding – another cross-curricular theme.

## Children and the environment

Jeff Hague has led the development of the conservation area in Doncaster Road Junior School over a period of 10 years. A distinctive feature of this area is the variety of habitats within it. One part represents moorland bog; another a grassy lowland; there is a small pond; and elsewhere a sandy dune.

Jeff's teaching role included a responsibility for children with special educational needs, but he encouraged all children to work in the conservation area, often in their 'own time'. Parents have also been drawn in. This is especially valuable as a chance to involve those parents who might not otherwise feel 'comfortable' coming into the classroom. Although vandalism is common enough in the area, it is remarkable that the school conservation area has remained unharmed.

One of the writers met Jeff Hague and 12 children, of mixed junior age range, one January afternoon. The intention was to talk in general terms with children about environmental education, and to learn something of their perceptions, knowledge and understanding of this area of the curriculum. The children all had a strong interest in the school conservation area work. They included four who were 'statemented' (i.e. identified as having special educational needs). They were thus a mixed-ability and a mixed-age group. It was pleasing to see the way in which they collaborated and worked together although they did not know each other well.

We sat in a ring around tables in the school library. After introductions we recognised that all present had an interest in environmental education. We then outlined to the children that we would be interested to hear their views about the environment.

The following are short extracts from the discussion, presented in sequence. They feature some of the initial responses of children to discussion points and questions which emerged. At some points in the discussion there was more teacher exposition, to clarify topics children had introduced. The initial intention had been to find out what children understood by the concepts of 'environment', 'conservation', and 'pollution' by introducing these words in turn. As it turned out children talked about both conservation and pollution when discussing what they understood by the word 'environment'.

The word 'environment' was written on the chalkboard.

*Teacher:* Imagine you have someone visiting from another country and they say to you 'what does this word "environment" mean?'

*Lennie:* Animals and trees and the things that are living.

*Laura:* Rocks and the space around us...

*Derek:* Conservation...

*Laura:* Land.

*Phil:* Caring about plants.

*Derek:* When people drop rubbish and other people come round ... and picks it up cause somebody threw their rubbish down without putting it in the bin.

*Teacher:* What do we call people who throw things down?

*Mary:* Litter bug.

*Teacher:* Good. Any other things about the environment or has everybody had a go?

*Lennie:* It's what's around us.

*Jeff:* Anybody think of anything else which has to do with the environment? What else can we say about the environment?

*Lennie:* Trees?

*Jeff:* Trees. Where are the trees?

*Lennie:* There on the grass.

*Jeff:* And where is the grass?

*Lennie:* On the concrete...

*Jeff:* Not actually on the concrete. So far we have the trees on the grass which are about us. But what else is there about us?

Carly: Soil.

Jeff: Soil. Yes, all about us there are lots of things growing in it. What else is there about us? David.

David: Mud.

Jeff: Let's start thinking not only just there, but let's start to think in other directions.

Laura: Air.

Jeff: Air, right. All the air and everything that is about us. What else?

Mary: Pollution.

Jeff: Pollution, all about us. What else is there about us? Look out of the window and see what is about us.

James: Life.

Jeff: Life of all sorts. Not only the plants and the animals. What else is there, that is about?

Carly: Insects.

Lennie: The atmosphere.

Laura: Us.

Jeff: Yes, us, and everything we do, everything which we have made, everything which your parents and your grandparents have made.

In this discussion we can see some of the key ideas about 'the environment' held by children in this mixed-ability and mixed-age group of juniors. Between them, and with some prompting, they listed elements of the global environmental system. We can note how the natural world first came to their minds: animals, trees, rocks, plants, soil, air. Some children offered more sophisticated notions of environment – 'the space around us' and 'what's around us'. With a little prompting one child came to remember 'us' – people – as elements in the environment.

It was interesting to see how quickly and naturally the children brought the words conservation and pollution into this discussion of environment. They already had an understanding of the interrelationship between these concepts.

Conservation and pollution were raised for further discussion.

Teacher: Conservation: what do you think conservation is to do with?

Charlie: Picking up litter.

James: Exploring the wildlife and nature.

Mary: Helping the animals, and replanting the gardens.

James: Planting new plants.

Lennie: Looking after trees.

Carly: Helping plants grow.

*Teacher:* How might we help plants grow, do you think Carly?
*Carly:* Take weeds out.

Again litter received an early mention when focusing discussion on conservation. The emphasis initially was again upon plant and animal life. Ensuing points of discussion that children brought in included 'filling up ponds' for frogs, the ozone layer, and tidying up streams.

We can appreciate from these fragments of discussion how these children have a basic familiarity with many key ideas in environmental education. Questions of environment, pollution, resource management, and of conservation, were within their current understanding. From that classroom discussion we can identify a basic four-fold categorisation of sources of environmental awareness.

First there is the school. Some of the children's thinking appears to have been influenced strongly by their learning experiences in the classroom and in school. Their immediate responses and thoughts are associated with the environmental topics which are part of the school curriculum for environmental education.

Second, beyond the classroom, the children have personal knowledge about other issues derived from their own observations. Some observations were local to home, for example pollution of the River Trym. Other knowledge was derived from memories of holidays, such as rubbish seen on Belgian beaches.

This can be linked to parents as a third source of environmental knowledge and understanding: 'my Dad said there was a lot of dirt in the sea' (why they were not allowed to swim at Sheerness).

Fourth, TV and other media are influential in enhancing environmental education by raising children's awareness of major environmental threats and hazards, perhaps supplementing lessons in school. During the discussion children volunteered ideas about equatorial rain forests, CFCs, and the ozone layer – all topics about which they have some elementary knowledge and understanding.

We can also see how they have a real concern for all elements demonstrating a caring attitude and a sense of responsibility. Thus, to the earlier components of environmental education of learning 'in', 'through' and 'about' the environment (illustrated by the enthusiastic response of Paula Knee's children), there is added the strand of 'learning for' the environment.

Environmental education is often seen as centring upon the 'natural environment', and aspects of the built environment. But for a fuller understanding children will learn how people, and the actions of people, are also very much part of our environment.

Thus environmental education not only fits well in a review of the position of humanities in the primary curriculum. It can also be a way of enriching the lives of young children, and helping them grow and learn more about 'what is special about being human'.

## Environmental education: a vehicle for personal and social education

In considering the nature of environmental education we have been thinking largely of cognitive aspects of learning. However, in addition to thinking about how children can learn 'in', 'through', and 'for' the environment, we need also to consider the contribution it provides for child-centred approaches supporting personal and social education. Linked with this how can environmental education help children with learning difficulties?

We can again draw upon some of the experiences of Jeff Hague to illustrate the potential of environmental education, when practised by experienced and sensitive teachers, to help children grow in confidence and self-esteem.

Jeff Hague recalled an event which opened his eyes in an unexpected way:

... it was an ex-approved school. We had a Naval watch system, and I was head of one of the watches. Now I was on duty one night, in the summer and we had various problems, mass break-outs, normal problems for that type of school. It was about half past nine, kids had all had their supper, the flag had been taken down, we had a bugle blowing and I was walking along the terrace. I looked up, and lined against the windows were loads of the boys. Which immediately makes one think there is SOME problem. Now these boys ... you never knew quite what was going to happen. I was sort of concerned so I went up, to try and appear as if I wasn't...."Come and look at this, Sir"... and they were looking at the sunset!

I would say probably half of the boys in the school were looking and enjoying a sunset across the Bristol Channel. The sun was sinking down behind the Welsh hills. It was a beautiful thing, but that these kids were so much enjoying this, was, I thought, quite incredible.

Jeff went on to describe how this experience stimulated his thinking about environmental education. The response of some rather challenging young people to the setting of the sun suggested that 'the environment' could be helpful to children experiencing a variety of difficulties and problems. Perhaps by being with animals, or working with plants, many more children might be helped to find interests, develop their self-esteem, and build relationships with others:

> I realised that there was an affinity between the countryside and wildlife, and youngsters with problems – identity problems, well-being problems.

The children included many who found it difficult to relate readily to others. Nevertheless by starting to get involved in environmental education, many children were helped to look beyond themselves and their immediate concerns. Environmental education also provided children with chances to work together. Once again Vygotskian principles of learning, and the importance of talk, were often in evidence as children were able to discuss together, and to gain from interacting in this way. It also provided opportunities for some children to assume a leading role at times when this might not have been expected – certainly not by their peers. Many practical elements of environmental education and problem solving involve such group work:

> …somebody who wasn't very strong physically would possibly develop the best plan. And he, or she, would perhaps be in control of half a dozen or so in a group…

During a dinner-hour chat over coffee, Jeff was prompted to recall memories of one particular pupil. These illustrate strikingly how environmental education can provide a medium for helping children with profound special educational needs.

*Interviewer:* I always remember the time you told us about the boy who could not communicate in class, but ended up addressing an audience in Bristol of about 1,200.

*Jeff:* Yes, Rex. Rex in particular I suppose, who was virtually mute, you couldn't tell him anything. If you did sort of scold him, slightly point out that something was not quite right, two plus two isn't five, he would disappear. He would sob his little heart out at the back of the classroom, under the table. It was a major problem. He didn't have any real skills apparent at the time, he couldn't read, he couldn't write and he really was in quite a bad way…

*Interviewer:* How old was he then?

*Jeff:* That would have been 8 years old. It was a case of trying to find some way of making contact. After a while I noticed that he was taking quite a considerable interest in the plants – a keen interest.

He was always wanting to put in seeds, take seeds out of their tray, put them into pots. I started working with the then deputy head.

I was in a hut just in the playground at the time and immediately opposite the deputy had her class. We worked out that he needed really to make contact with other people. He was beginning to make contact with me. He needed to make contact with some others in his class. We wanted to move him in and out, so she used to be ready and I would send Rex across with a potted plant to her, and I'd say 'It's alright Rex. I'll watch you all the way. You just cross a little bit of garden to the double doors'. And almost straight away he's knocking the door. He wouldn't go in – he would wait...I could see him when he felt settled, she would take the glass from him and then we developed this movement of plants. He would go across and collect a plant because it needed watering. He would look after it for a week or so, and then he'd take some cuttings across to her and he would go across and collect the cuttings from her. So he was going backwards and forwards, and making contact.

Jeff went on to describe Rex's gradual social integration into various aspects of school life – including drama classes and sports activities – through the increased confidence he attained in nurturing the plants.

The punch line really is his last summer term. He was on stage at the Colston Hall on his own. And I saw him a couple of years ago, and he's qualified as a chef now, and he was working at that time at the [Major Hotel]. Initially you could put it all down to plants, because at the beginning, the little chinks in his armour were opened up by working with plants.

These accounts illustrate the potential for environmental education when imaginatively used as a vehicle for learning. Children working in a school conservation area might not only be developing some useful scientific knowledge and understanding. These learning activities might also blossom into many exciting and rewarding outcomes for the children; for parents who can become actively involved in school life perhaps for the first time; and for the teacher concerned with the needs of individual children, and for members of the school community. Like Rex, many children have been helped to grow in confidence and self-esteem through the medium of environmental education.

Environmental education is a curriculum focus which is very strongly 'people centred'. It is therefore appropriately placed within the primary humanities curriculum. Not only does it contribute to the cognitive domain – it also has great potential for developing learning in the affective domain, in aesthetics and in personal and social education. It also has 'humanising' potential for individual children; it can help them to know what it is to be human. It can foster a sense of achievement and of 'self-worth'. Through practical investigations and problem solving, children can be encouraged to work collaboratively, and to learn from each other in a social context. Vygotskian principles again shed light on our appreciation of this process. This collaborative way of working is shared not only across other areas of primary humanities, but can also be encouraged in other curriculum areas. Science investigations, for example, can be so organised that children work alongside each other under the direction of the teacher. In doing this they are helped to grow as individuals, as well as developing vital interpersonal skills.

The discussion of environmental education in this chapter has dealt with children's learning when responding to and working in their local environment. We have also recognised that they can have an appreciation of some global issues. We have seen how environmental education can support personal and social education, and can sometimes help parents to share more actively in school life.

In the last part of this chapter two other questions will be briefly explored, as part of the backcloth to environmental education in the primary curriculum. These questions are:

(a) How might children be encouraged to appreciate the social justice dimension within global environmental education?
(b) What is meant by environmentalism?

## Environmental education: global environmental education and questions of social justice

Most of us recognise that there are costs – which will affect us as individuals – when seeking to solve environmental problems. People have needs which must be met simply to survive. We use a whole variety of resources, from various parts of the globe, to meet those basic physical needs – food, shelter, warmth. However, many of us have been able to share in overall increasing standards of living over the last two or three decades. In the UK this has not applied to the poorest. Those with incomes in the lowest 10% bracket are no better off than in the late 1960s, according to a research report from Bristol University (*Guardian*, 1994a). However prosperity, generally speaking, has grown, and even if it is only the top 10% richest whose real incomes have shot up by 60% on average since 1979, very many of us we have unconsciously increased our activity as consumers. This increase in economic activity has had the effect, among others, of making greater demands upon the earth's resources, which are often strictly limited. Inevitably there is a growing strain upon the ability of the earth's life support system to meet our apparently ever-increasing demands and expectations as Rachel Carson gave warning over 30 years ago (Carson, 1963).

Commonly recognised environmental issues such as rain forest clearance, reduction of sewage in British coastal waters, reductions in use of CFCs, renovating the chemically weathered columns of the Parthenon, reducing sulphur emission from fossil burning power stations are all likely to hit our pockets one way or another. Some of these 'problems' we may feel we are distanced from – we might not choose to eat beefburgers in any case, and thus we may not have a stake in the farming of beef cattle in cleared rain-forest areas. Similarly we may not bathe along the south coast (especially if we take our own children off to foreign holidays with clean hotel swimming pools and so do not need to worry about British sewage levels). By and large we can appreciate both the financial costs, and other costs (such as loss of choice, convenience or amenity) in ameliorating if not solving environmental problems. As such we can then lend or withhold our support to measures to improve or 'save the environment'.

The financial costs that are part and parcel of being responsible 'for the environment' are readily acknowledged. Indeed, the increase in VAT on domestic fuel introduced in April 1994 by the British Government was claimed to be an environmental tax to help conserve energy. What is not so readily acknowledged are the social and political dimensions of our use of resources – who loses out? In the processes which provide us with various goods and services, who suffers and who is being exploited? From time to time news items inform us of the harsh working conditions of some factory operatives in sweatshops in some southeast Asian countries. The people are working in these conditions to provide cheaply priced garments on sale in our high-street stores. Christian Aid, Oxfam and other non-governmental organisations also inform us about child labour being exploited in villages in India to produce attractive carpets or shoes, which can also be very competitively priced by UK high-street standards.

We saw in Chapter 3 how 7–9-year-old children in Pilning School, studying 'people and place' in South Africa, had a basic sense of social justice, of 'what is fair', when they were discussing aid and trade. They supported the case for paying 'fair prices' for goods exchanged in our interdependent world.

John Huckle (1988) writing about environmental education, describes how the power position enjoyed by the rich and strong is maintained at the expense of the costs, environmental and other, borne by the weak:

> Decisions taken by powerful minorities generally mean that it is the poor and powerless who suffer most from environmental problems as polluted water, damp housing, the shortage of fuelwood, flooding as a result of deforestation, and inner city crime...verbal abuse, sexual harassment, vandalism, mugging ...caused by and result from a lack of environmental well-being.

Huckle argues the case for environmental education having a broader canvas than just concerns about the natural environment, the built environment and the consumption of the earth's resources. Environmental education certainly is concerned with questions of the rate at which resources are used, and the uses to which they are put. However, another essential part of the overall equation is the question of how those goods are distributed – indeed shared – among people in our immediate community, as well as in the wider global community.

Some of the ways in which children can build on their awareness and understanding of social dimensions of environmental concerns was illustrated in talking with 9–11-year-old children in Hambrook Primary School. They had been engaged in a class topic on 'Homelessness'. Initially this topic was seen in terms of humanities generally and as having particular relevance to religious education and moral education. Subsequently the pertinence to environmental education was recognised in the concepts and ideas being expressed by the children. The values being clarified by the children were again central to those expressed in the study of humanities.

In groups of four or five, children were asked about their work and activities on this topic of 'homelessness'. Many of them had some first-hand encounter with those who are homeless, seeing them on the streets in the town centre. They showed a keen appreciation of the complexity of the problem of homelessness and of some of the difficulties of trying to meet those needs. It was also impressive how readily these children, as a whole class, had responded by trying to be 'people who did something'. They sought active ways of helping those in greater need than themselves. It was also evident how strongly many of these 9–11-year-old children could identify with the homeless, and those who begged on the streets. They could vividly imagine what it would be like to have to live on the streets.

The following is an extract of a conversation with one group of five children as they spoke about the homeless and how they tried to help them. Some of the subsequent quotations were from talking with other groups children.

*Teacher/interviewer:* What do we understand or mean by the homeless?

*Bella:* They haven't got anywhere to live so they live in the streets.

*Interviewer:* Bella's saying nowhere to live, live on the streets. Anybody else add to that?

*Interviewer:* They haven't got a home.

*Jamie:* They haven't got a job.

*Tim:* They haven't got any money.

*Interviewer:* Have you all seen some people who are homeless? So Cliff where have you seen some?

*Cliff:* Down the centre.

*Interviewer:* In the town centre. And what are they doing?

*Tim:* Sitting down in the streets.

*Karen:* Ragged.

*Jamie:* Asking for money.

*Interviewer:* Ragged, sitting on streets, asking for money. Anything more?

*Tim:* They live in cardboard boxes sometimes, you see a row of them in like the Leisure Centre.

*Interviewer:* Yes, often they may live in a cardboard box.

*Jamie:* We've got a viaduct and they, used to 'cause now it's a nature reserve, they used to go down there.

*Tim:* They've got a little hut.

*Interviewer:* Oh is that near Hambrook?

*Tim:* Yeh.

*Bella:* In Staple Hill at the car park round the back, there's this little shack and they used to keep things round there.

*Tim:* They put buckets outside and put 'help the homeless and hungry if you have any change'.

*Interviewer:* That's of course Staple Hill, which is outside of the centre. Why do we think people have become homeless? Have they always been homeless?

*Bella:* No, because usually they've had a argument at home and they want to run away.

*Cliff:* They're feeling bad about something.

*Jamie:* ...and fed up.

*Karen:* They may be on drugs.

*Interviewer:* Yes, perhaps get involved with drugs.

| | |
|---|---|
| *Bella:* | Some people have a problem with other things, like some reasons why they can't get a job. People won't let them in as lodgers because they had a problem in the past, and they still think they've got the problem, but really they are trying to forget it …if they can't get a job. |
| *Interviewer:* | So they can't get a job easily. What effect does that have? |
| *Jamie:* | They're living on the streets. |
| *Cliff:* | Their families all died and they haven't got any money, so like they go on the streets. |
| *Interviewer:* | Yes, maybe they are left without a family to support them. |
| *Jamie:* | Another reason they can't get a job is nobody will give them a reference. So they can't get anywhere to live because they can't get a job, because they need an address to get a job. |
| *Interviewer:* | So it's what we might call a… |
| *Jamie:* | Vicious circle. |
| *Interviewer:* | That's the plight of those who are homeless. Now then, some of you have been more actively involved in this. Think back to when you started. How did it get going? How did it start? |
| *Bella:* | We tried to think of a way to stop homeless. |
| *Interviewer:* | What sort of things did you come up with? |
| *Karen:* | We thought about getting loads of money together. |
| *Cliff:* | Getting loads of money and building a shelter. They could stay for about 2 years because then they come and depend on the shelter too much. |
| *Interviewer:* | So getting money together, providing a shelter, but you're aware that sometimes you don't want to supply too much because it might be difficult for people to do some things for themselves. Bella what were you going to say? |
| *Bella:* | Miss Tribe came in…well first of all she talked to us and then we wrote a rough letter off to somebody who could stop it. We were thinking about how different shelters could be set up. And how we could… |
| *Karen:* | …get them food. |
| *Jamie:* | …write letters to people. |
| *Interviewer:* | So we're talking about shelter, providing food and so on. Now what has happened since? You mentioned letters. What sort of letters? |
| *Tim:* | We sent to John Major and we sent to the Queen. |

> And we had one back from both of them.
>
> *Interviewer:* Why did you send letters, do you think, to John Major and the Queen?
>
> *Karen:* Because they've got the money.
>
> *Cliff:* They've got the power too.
>
> *Bella:* They're important so people believe in them.
>
> *Interviewer:* They're important and their views would be...
>
> *Jamie:* Important to the rest of the people.
>
> *Tim:* They can order people about.

In this discussion the children show that they have a sound appreciation of the circumstances of many homeless people and of the restricted access they have to environmental resources enjoyed by the great majority of people in society. Some of the knowledge was from first-hand observation. In the words of another child:

> I went to the Hippodrome with my cousin, and there was loads. We went past the Big Burger King and there were like five people out there.

The causes of homelessness, the complexity of defining the homeless, and differing views of the authenticity of their needs were also voiced. Problems faced at home, depression, and drugs, were mentioned by children in the group talking above. In similar vein a child in another group suggested:

> And sometimes they might have had some sort of financial difficultly, so they can't pay the rent if they have a flat or the mortgage. So they have to get chucked out. They can't get a job to get money because they haven't got a house to get the address. People don't like having them. And they can't get a house they can't get a job. It's just one big circle.

Some of the children showed an awareness of the ways in which study of the homeless was problematic. First there was a question about people who beg and appear to be homeless, but might not in fact need to beg:

> Yes but they're not, some of them aren't homeless, some of them are and they just want more money. They make about £100 a day.

The source for this viewpoint was not established but might have been from classroom discussion, from home or the media.

Other children based their reservations about the need for financial help on their observations of those they had seen on the street:

> They've got earrings, and they smoke as well, and they cost a lot of money. They must have some money. Quite a lot.

It was impressive to note that although the children had been moved, in the course of their study, to act on behalf of the homeless, they had also been encouraged to ask questions, to maintain a critical approach, and not simply accept that there was only one way of interpreting the phenomenon of homelessness.

Just as striking was the ability of the children to empathise with those who were homeless. With this came the feeling that they should respond in some way. Some voiced their concern simply, like Emma: 'I wouldn't like it if I were homeless', when asked why she had been doing things on their behalf. Two or three children expressed their values in relation to social justice and fairness more graphically, like Clare:

> So it's not fair really having homes and loads and loads of facilities. I lie in my bed at night – it's dark, cold and raining outside, and I think of them cold, hungry... out on the streets with sleeping bags. And I'm there in bed nice and warm.

She was able to draw strong comparisons between her home environment, and the different experiences of the homeless on the streets. The value judgement 'It's not fair' was made by several children during the course of discussions.

The difficulties of providing the appropriate kind of help was recognised by children. In particular they noted that people should be encouraged to have some independence where possible:

> ...it isn't a good thing to give them money; they'll rely on you;
> ...sometimes we have to be careful – they become too dependent on you.

Children were also able to reflect upon the feelings which had prompted them to try to act on behalf of the homeless. Again, some of these are basic humanitarian attitudes and values, which presumably would not only be promoted in humanities, but more widely, outside as well as inside school. When asked why they had tried to take some action children were able to describe their attitudes in various ways:

> ...to help other people.
> – It makes you feel better helping people.
> – It's like it's personal to you. You feel really happy when you get something. It's even better to give something.

During some of the conversations questions of selfishness, and of conscience were introduced. Karen reflected on her home situation as an only child:

> About what someone was talking about earlier, about

conscience. I'm an only child in a family, and sometimes a younger brother or sister is sort of like a conscience really. 'Cause if you were really eating loads of things that were really bad for you, and you just eat and eat and eat, and if you didn't have another brother or sister there to share things with you, you'd just get so fat you'd blow up. It's not necessarily just food – it's the way we live; selfishness with things like TV, and things like that.

Interviewer: So you're saying that if you have got a brother or sister you have to share things more often. So it's a good thing to share, do we all agree? It's a good thing to share. Bella?

Bella: Yeah, but with my sister...what if she doesn't share them with you? Can I do this? No. Tough.

Bella here brought us back to earth and the realities of family life, with her views on sharing between brothers and sisters.

Children were asked what had made them, or encouraged them, to write their letters to the Queen, John Major, and to local supermarket chains. There were varied responses:

- It's not fair
...to do something about it
...To make some difference at least, even if it won't make much difference, it could help a little bit, because if more people would help I'm sure there wouldn't be so many homeless people.

As they discussed their active involvement the children revealed how this

---

*Hambrook School*
*Moorend RD*
*Hambrook*
*Bristol*

*To Mr Major,*

  *My name is ——— and I am ten years of age.*
*I have grown quite concerned about the growning number of people out on the streets. Around broadmead - close to wear I 'live, I have noticed quite a big increase in the recent three years of the people living on the streets in broadmead.*
*I know you are very, very busy most of the time but if you could find some time to maybe put up some shelters to give some homeless somewhere to sleep and maybe give them some food and drink.*
*I know you have hardly any spare time but any little thing can help*  *THANKYOU YOURS SINCERELY*

---

**Figure 5.2** Letter to the Prime Minister

activity had made them even more interested in the topic, and had increased their motivation.

> We found it a bit boring at first, 'cause we thought we were just writing the letters to put in our folders, but then, we didn't realise they would actually be sent off.
> Then we knew we were going to send them off, and we started getting letters back. And then we got excited.

Figure 5.2 shows a letter from one of the children to the Prime Minister. When this discussion was recorded, the children were just preparing to visit the supermarket to choose provisions for the homeless. They had sought advice from Shelter regarding the most appropriate types of food. They thought that the supermarkets had responded very positively to the needs of the homeless, and were satisfied with the response from the Queen.

The Government seemingly could try harder:

> Now the Government, most of the time they put the taxes up. They should give it to people who can't even buy a carton of milk.

The work on homelessness raised varied issues for them; questions of power, of social justice, of responsibility to others, of good neighbourliness. They were also expressing feelings and attitudes about others in greater need than themselves. When asked they did not immediately think of this as involving religious education. This topic also brought in questions about 'the environment' and what the 'environment' constituted for those who did not have a home of their own. The topic concerns inequalities: how are resources used by society at large, and how equitable is the distribution of them.

## Environmentalism and environmental education

As noted above, environmental education generally has support across the political and ideological spectrum. It can be assumed that most people do have some awareness of potential environmental problems. If we are aware of environmental issues, and feel that some sort of action should be taken to reduce their impact or alleviate their pressures, then we can count ourselves as 'environmentalists'. As environmentalists we would be in favour of environmental education in some form.

Accepting that such education should feature in primary school classrooms, what sort of environmental education would it be? Would it be more local than global? Should it be largely passive learning, or involve elements of action? Would it be essentially about 'them', or would it recognise that it also involves 'us', our chosen lifestyles and common assumptions of ever-increasing standards of living? What are the basic values we hold about people and planet earth which would underpin our curriculum for environmental education?

In seeking to clarify our own values about our place in the world and in turn any responsibility we feel we might have to the earth and its peoples, we can usefully reflect upon the two-fold set of viewpoints distinguished by O'Riordan (1989). The simple distinction which O'Riordan makes is between:

(a) The 'nature as nurture' mode of thought, which places humankind in its ecological setting, and recognises the need to treat our environment with respect and understanding, and

(b) The 'nature as usufruct' mode of thought, which sees nature and all it provides as there to be fully exploited, since the scientific know-how of the experts will solve any possible problems. After all it, i.e. know-how, has always done so in the past...hasn't it?

O'Riordan also highlights the way in which some people are instrumental in the processes of exploitation. This perception fits closely with the view of the exercise of power and of discrimination against the poor, which was outlined above, with reference to the homeless. He writes about the 'exploitation of the weak, whether weak (is) the natural world or lesser mortals' (O'Riordan, 1989:78).

O'Riordan postulates two basic responses to the natural world. On the one hand, there are those who see no constraints upon how we use our global environment; and on the other hand, there are those who teach that we should recognise our stewardship of planet earth. There are many worldviews which recognise a God, or a God-like dimension to creation, but some are framed in a 'nurturing mode' and others in a 'manipulative mode'. He suggests 'The God metaphor stands for the force of creation, a superhuman and unimaginable phenomenon lying beyond human intelligence and consciousness' (1989:82).

In the nurturing mode, God created the world, and then human beings. This is in accord with the Judaeo-Christian creation myth (seeking insights into *why* we are here in the world, rather than *how* it actually started) as told in the first chapter in Genesis. In this worldview, we are due to have great reverence and respect for nature and to exercise more care in using natural resources. In part this outlook has regard for what is left to future generations, as well as how resources are distributed among present-day peoples. By way of contrast, in the manipulative mode, human beings have a God-given right to reign supreme over nature. Constraints are not recognised as we go about the business of exploiting what the earth offers, whether through the consumption of materials, or through the labour and industry of other people. In any case, as humans who are at the top of the heap, we have the wisdom, allied to increasingly sophisticated technology, to design an ever-improving environmental in which to live. Or so we might be tempted to believe.

This is of course an abbreviated summary of some of the notions of environmentalism put forward by O'Riordan. Our personal world view might or might not find the notion of God to be helpful or relevant. Nevertheless the simple question of where we, as humans, fit into the environmental scheme of things (God-given or otherwise) can have resonance in classroom situations. Children are capable of opening up new vistas, or lines of enquiry, which can surprise their teacher.

Emma Dangerfield, a PGCE student, was working with 8-year-old children. She introduced a science lesson on animals and wildlife by using a card game to promote discussion about animal needs for survival. She wrote in her teaching log:

Many children had strong feelings about unacceptable animal usage, including circuses, research, the ivory trade, and performing animals. I was very surprised that some of these feelings were so deeply felt, and shall try never to assume that children do not consider these issues.

I was also surprised that some children brought up the Christian creation story as justification for treating animals fairly, as God created animals as well as humans. (April 26 1994)

The gradations of environmentalism can be extended from the two-fold division of 'nature as nurture' and 'nature as usufruct'. O'Riordan (p.85)

| Environmental Viewpoints Ecocentric  Technocentric | | | |
|---|---|---|---|
| **Gaianism** | **Communalism** | **Accommodation** | **Interventionalism** |
| upholds the rights of nature | co-operative movement<br><br>use of renewable resources | being adaptable<br><br>assessing and evaluating resource use | complete faith in the application of science |

**Figure 5.3** Environmentalist viewpoints (Adapted from O'Riordan, 1989:85)

refers to these as environmental ideologies in proposing the following worldviews summarized in simple form in Figure 5.3.

We can use this model to check our own environmentalist stance, and hence the kind of environmental education that we would think desirable in the primary curriculum.

The key dimension (ecocentrism–technocentrism) concerns the balance to be struck between technological solutions and ecological considerations in seeking to respond to environmental issues. Where would we place our own viewpoints on this model?

At one end of the spectrum, heavily technocentric, there are those who believe modern science has all the answers; these include the technological fixers. All they have to do is intervene in the natural world as and when appropriate. The accommodators are also confident that technology can produce solutions, but are prepared to be adaptable, and to monitor global situations to take precautionary action.

The ecocentrists believe technology has insufficient answers to the problems we face; that the scale of modern industrial enterprise and of central state authority is such that the requisite sensitive responses to environmental problems cannot be made. They are critical of assumptions of ever-increasing growth. Communalists, respecting nature, emphasise co-operative measures and using renewable resources. At the far end of this continuum (Gaianism) there are those who uphold the rights of nature, and argue that humans should make minimal demands upon natural resources.

As individuals (and as educators) we can consider where we stand on the scale, asking ourselves whether there is a good fit between our proclaimed environmentalist position and our day-to-day lifestyle? Further, what are the implications for environmental education in schools with regard to these different value positions? Most value positions would encourage children to be active in some way with regard to environmental issues and concerns. The need for teachers to think about how children can develop a sense of responsibility for people and environments, and for taking appropriate action, is advocated by the OECD, among other authorities: 'A prime purpose of Environmental Education is to give people the determination to act with a view to solving or preventing environmental problems' (OECD, 1993:28). Some of these questions of children and citizenship are developed more fully in the next chapter. The teaching of humanities is not made any easier by the inescapable conclusion that it involves children working with controversial issues. The importance of children being able to engage openly with such issues in environmental education was affirmed by the DES (1989b:3) when writing about 'informed concern' for the environment:

Environmental issues are of genuine personal concern to many pupils and can act as a useful means of exploring moral, social and political values. Pupils should be equipped to bring to the study of controversial issues – environmental and others – a respect for evidence and understanding of other's concerns and a growing realisation that choices are rarely clear-cut....

to avoid bias and indoctrination it is necessary for young people to acquire an informed and critical understanding of all the views held about such issues and an appreciation of how actions and decisions now and later affect the environment.

O'Riordan (1989:91) having reviewed the claims for environmental education as learning in, learning about, and learning for the environment concludes, decisively, on the primacy of the last of these:

education *for* the environment remains the critical objective for Environmental Education.

## Summary

We can thus appreciate the strong and natural links which environmental education has with geography and religious education as well as with history. Space does not allow a fuller consideration of the claims for environmental education to be centred in the humanities, although the classroom examples given in this chapter do illustrate how children are aware of the social justice dimension within environmental education. Children can also, sometimes, be more open to moral and religious questions than many adults, who are inclined to place environmental education firmly under the banner of science in the curriculum. Children, less used to having to justify classroom learning in terms of subject areas, can provide an alternative viewpoint here. Environmental education essentially involves people and their livelihoods and so sometimes raises questions of social justice. Children also cast themselves in the role of 'the person(s) who did something', and work co-operatively to take some form of positive action. The themes of children exercising responsibility and of taking action are developed further in the following chapter on citizenship.

# CHAPTER 6

# Education for Citizenship in a Changing World

## Introduction

When is a citizen not a citizen? This question may sound like the beginning of a joke but it is meant to make a serious point about everyday life in a democracy. We could add the question 'where is a citizen not a citizen?' and interject with the short answers 'never and nowhere'.

We do need positive answers, however, and in this chapter we will be exploring the 'when and where' of citizenship and citizenship education. Citizens act out their everyday lives in a range of different worlds, some of them more public, some of them less so. Citizens move from domestic situations, to work-place institutions, to the market-place and many other public arenas. These are all locations where their interactions and decisions are significant and have effects and where their principles are open to scrutiny. A citizenship education programme for children will concern itself with such everyday situations. It needs to start with the familiar personal and inter-personal worlds of the school and classroom and then spread its focus to the wider world.

In this chapter we will also explore the 'what' and the 'how' of citizenship and citizenship education. The term citizenship is complex and understanding it includes discussion of rights, freedoms and responsibilities. Understanding citizenship education also includes discussion of values underpinning active citizenship.

## Tales of citizenship at home, at school and in society

A warning was issued through 'Points West' – a television news programme which is well known to citizens in the South West region of England. We were told of the dangers of action that some local people were taking – as concerned citizens – about the routing of a new bypass road through part of what is left of the green and pleasant landscape of England. We were shown moving pictures of the bulldozers which belonged to the road building citizens and not far from these mighty machines, the protesting citizens – a distance, it seemed on the screen, of approximately 1cm. All parent citizens were warned of the dangers of such locations and scenes to children. It was, after all, the summer holidays and children citizens were beginning to take an active interest in an issue which, although resolved through the processes of the law courts, was still generating heartfelt and bitter concern. This concern was being well advertised through news broadcasts and local newspapers. The controversy was still raging.

We did not receive news via the television on that evening about another group of children citizens who were protesting in support of the road building. This story was reported in one of the local newspapers, *The Evening Post*. A photograph showed the children wearing gas masks for safety though this precaution taken on this one occasion would not be sufficient to offset the damage done during their short lives by the fumes from the heavy traffic on its way from Chippenham to Bath. For these children's homes were placed right next to the busy trunk road in the village which was due to be bypassed. The planning of this bypass had been the product of 20 years of struggle by local citizens. The placard which the children were carrying read simply: 'SAVE US, NOT THE GRASS'

This short account raises some interesting questions about citizenship education and provides some insights into the complexities of a working democracy and the limits of democratic procedures. It reminds us that the ability to handle and understand controversial issues is an essential part of preparation for active participation in a democracy. It also provides an example of the process by which we learn about citizenship – by being a citizen. As citizens we all (children included) learn from watching and reading the news on a daily basis. We also learn by active involvement and interaction with other citizens in our daily lives. Such interactions are usually at a personal level or, in the work-place, at an institutional level but this does not mean that the process should be any less democratic or less principled. Such day by day interactions are not newsworthy but they do none the less involve us in decision making about significant issues with other citizens.

A central argument in this chapter will be that many aspects of our personal lives are a part of our political lives. For example, decisions about what we are going to eat, where we are going to buy it or grow it, who is going to cook it and what energy supply we are going to use for that cooking, are all citizenship issues which have implications far beyond the domestic and institutional contexts where food is prepared and eaten.

Such a view of citizenship underlines the significance of the role of the teacher in a democratic political system. As teachers we have responsibility for structuring the social world of the schools which for many children are their first experience of institutional life, the first public context within which their experiences and behaviours will be tested.

We do not have to travel far into any school to realise that citizenship education is around every corner.

In one school for children with emotional and behavioural difficulties the headteacher explains that it has been a challenging day. It had started with an incident with a catapult. A very powerful catapult had been ill-advisedly brought to school by a child with the result that it was looked after first by a teacher, later by the headteacher and finally by the police at the police station. This succinct account conceals the emotional dimensions of the event, the anxieties, the fears, the anger, the relief and the frustration. It is a story that could have ended when the child ran home. The story was still unfolding even at the end of the day when teachers were attempting as responsible professionals to resolve the matter and bring the child back into the community of the school.

This incident was not the only challenging event of the day. Other quieter but similar stories were being acted out all the time. An observation of one child during a half hour period just before the end of the day revealed the following pattern:

Mike is quarrelling with another child over playground equipment... Mike is now calming down through talking with a General Assistant [GA]...Mike is now sitting contentedly next to the same GA during circle time...Mike is very animated about a picture which he has coloured in and will be taking home...Mike has been given responsibility to collect in the chairs in the Hall ...Mike is riding on the wheeled chair carrier in the Hall as if it is a scooter...Mike appears not to have heard another child telling him not to ride on the wheeled chair carrier in the Hall...Mike is quarrelling with the child who is telling him not to ride the wheeled chair carrier...Mike is fighting with this same child

about who is allowed to use the wheeled chair carrier...Mike is
calming down through talking with a teacher before getting on
the school bus to go home.

These are situations and predicaments which teachers and headteachers
from both special and mainstream schools can recognise. An important
consideration is that they were probably the most significant experiences
of the working day for those involved. The teachers and children would
certainly have continued to think about them and perhaps discuss them on
their way home and at home. Issues of rights, responsibilities, freedom
and justice were invoked and for the children the learning involved was
crucial to their development as social human beings.

The socialisation of children in the classroom and playground is an
important feature of the work of any group of teachers. Schools have
adopted many different strategies which encourage participation by all
concerned, including the children, for example by the establishment of a
school's council. A visit to another school, a mainstream primary school,
provides some examples of professional concern for and responsiveness
to this dimension of citizenship education.

On arrival a visitor is struck by the care and attention which has
been taken over the development and maintenance of the school
playground. This is an old school yard whose hard floor surfaces
and rectilinear walls have been softened and made more
aesthetically pleasing through the structured involvement of the
children's energies and imagination over a period of years. The
new environment now includes distinct areas which are
recognised by the children – a walled garden with sculptures,
paintings and plants, a painted tile mural, a herb garden and a
range of floor markings in different areas which are stimulating
different kinds of imaginative play. Inside the headteacher's
office some children report on the work done to collect litter
from a particular part of the school site. They volunteer to
organise the continuation of the work on the next day and
receive 'I Care for the Environment' stickers. They are pleased
with this achievement.

Meanwhile a senior teacher is working to resolve social and
injury issues which have arisen over lunchtime. She is making
careful records of such incidents and is making reference to the
'Good Behaviour Policy' which is recognised by the children and
staff alike and which is supporting the process of making
judgements and reaching agreements. The lunchtime
supervisory staff are joining in the discussion. In some cases
there is an immediate communication with parents. The
supervisory staff are relaying communications about decisions

which have been reached to other members of staff.

The significance of such practice had been noticed by the children. An interview with a group of 10-year-old children revealed that although they found it hard to specify the meaning of the term citizenship, they were able to articulate very clearly about how the safety and welfare of children in the school was assured. They discussed the risks for people in the outside world, in particular homelessness and the dangers of pollution and traffic. They contrasted this world outside with the environment of the school and provided an unplanned tour of the school noticeboards which variously encourage parental involvement, safe conduct and the saving of energy and which provide information about HELPLINES and about the procedures of the 'Good Behaviour Policy'.

These observations illustrate that school is one of the places where citizens are citizens. They are citizens in the playgrounds, the corridors, the headteachers' rooms, the classrooms, the borderline territories of the school gates and the buses which take children home. For children these are all important sites for learning about the complexity of social behaviour because they are (relatively) safe and controlled environments in which they have opportunity to interact with a range of people. The responsibility of the teacher in this respect is reflected in the current interest shown by the inspectorate in the ethos of the schools which they visit.

It is not surprising, however, that in spite of this children found it difficult to articulate the meaning of the term citizenship. This is a complex term which has engaged the likes of lawyers, philosophers, sociologists, historians, geographers and politicians (amongst others) in a protracted and ongoing debate. The complexity of this debate will need to be addressed prior to an attempt to identify aims for citizenship education.

## Conceptions of active citizenship

The case studies referred to above have been about conflicts (or potential conflicts) between citizens. They all include issues of social justice, rights, freedom and responsibility. We have seen these issues emerge in other case studies in other chapters, for example in relation to curriculum work which children undertook on homelessness (*see* Chapter 5) and on South Africa (*see* Chapter 3). Many other examples could have been given, for example, conflicts of interest over gender roles at home and in society, over trading agreements between individuals and groups, over the use of different energy sources or the treatment by humans of animals – all issues connected to the preparation of food. There are many more such conflicts of interest; they are all the concern of citizens. The conflicts are more complex because they occur in a plural society and in a rapidly changing world in which agreement over underlying values is not always easy to find.

These scenarios illustrate that citizenship can be conceptualised at both personal and political levels and that consistency between these levels is both possible and desirable. Clough and Menter (1993) have referred to another kind of conceptual distinction related to citizenship – the legalistic and the humanistic:

> By legalistic we refer to the definition of citizenship within the law of a nation or supra-nation, such as the European Community. By humanistic we are referring more to the qualities which describe being a citizen, particularly taking responsibility for one's behaviour and actions. In a democratic society the two forms of citizenship should interconnect and be complementary. In Britain this complementarity is seen to break down when different groups of citizens have widely different life chances and life experiences.

We do not have to look far to see examples of such a breakdown. The experience of minority ethnic groups who are subjected to abuse has already been referred to in Chapter 4. This is a phenomenon which is readily observable in other European countries, and, according to recent research, is on the increase in Bristol (SARI, 1994). There are cases too where the legal framework is seen to operate against the interests of some groups. Individual citizens and some groups of citizens continue to take direct action in protest against the Criminal Justice Bill 1994 which will cause increased inequity of treatment for travelling communities as well as for other groups.

Other important conceptual distinctions can be made in definitions of citizenship. Cole *et al.* (1990/91) offer a distinction between individual and nationalist citizenship on the one hand and social and internationalist citizenship on the other. The former has been a key feature of 1980s Britain and was well illustrated by Prime Minister Major's idea of a 'Citizen's Charter'. At the extreme end of this conception the citizen becomes a consumer, an actor in the market place, and little consideration is given to responsibilities. Political parties on the left and right of the political spectrum have long been aware of inevitable tensions between the free marketeer and the responsible citizen. There is increasing doubt about the degree of responsibility assumed by consumers with access to free choice in a liberal market. A more social approach to citizenship has been a feature of socialist countries, past and present. Citizens are encouraged not only to take responsibility for their own actions, but also to consider the effects of these actions on others, indeed on the whole society.

It is evident to those who live within a democracy and to those who are able to observe democracies at work from the outside that the simple adoption of democratic procedures is not sufficient on its own to create a society where justice and fairness prevail. Although 'the people rule', power is not usually evenly distributed. Even if power was evenly distributed, it would still be possible for the 'people to rule' in an unjust and harmful way towards themselves and other societies. The central issues within active democratic systems are concerned with rights, freedoms and responsibilities. The balance between these is subject to constant change. In one society a particular group may have to struggle, perhaps for a long time, to gain freedoms and rights for themselves. In another society another group may have to struggle to maintain those freedoms and rights which have been won.

The rights in themselves will be varied – including economic rights, social rights, cultural rights, civil rights, political rights, environmental rights and individual rights. The same is true of freedoms, which include freedom of thought, conscience and religion, freedom of opinion and expression, freedom of peaceful assembly and to join a trade union, freedom from unlawful attacks on honour and reputation and the freedom of movement and residence. A central concern is the universality of these rights and freedoms so that they are equally accessible to all without fear of discrimination. A means to try to protect rights and freedoms for all citizens is through reference to relevant Conventions on Human Rights, for example the 1950 *European Convention on Human Rights* or the more recent 1989 *UN Convention on the Rights of the Child*. Such conventions include legal mechanisms which attempt to offer protection and the latter covers half of the world's populations – namely all those children under 18 years of age.

It is important also to consider the difference between national and global conceptions of citizenship. The concept of nation and nation state is particularly complex and has been the subject of discussion in an ERASMUS programme shared by universities across the European Community focusing on education for citizenship in a new Europe (ERASMUS ICP 2180). A discussion paper provided by Bereket Yebio a participant in this network, draws attention to some essential distinctions:

> Individuals in society can belong to a group sharing common historical, cultural, linguistic, ethnic or religious backgrounds. Such markers of shared identity are varied and can take many forms. Groups with such shared

identities can be found within a nation or across the borders of nations. This illustrates how difficult it is to define what national identity is. The term nation can refer to a group of people who share markers of identity and are indigenous inhabitants of a geographical territory. It can also refer to a geographical territory, recognised on a international legal basis by other national states. These are enclosed by boundaries which are subject to change following wars, treaties and agreements. What is the position of the many indigenous minorities living within and between nation states? The Kurdish peoples are such a group. Can they be regarded as a nation?

There are few conclusions to be drawn from this discussion except that nation states cannot be a permanent base for peoples' identities and that there is a great likelihood that several nations or groups will be present within a national state. This poses a problem for citizenship education programmes in schools which are based on conceptions of national citizenship. Which national identity should the citizenship education programme promote? And how could such a process avoid a denial of a positive self-image of the 'out group' and the imposition of the values of the 'in group'. A different conception of citizenship education based on ideas of nation would be a form of multi-national/intercultural education which recognised the plural nature of all societies.

The need for citizenship education at global and international levels is as pressing as ever. There are increasing numbers of developing democracies both world wide and across Europe. These are increasingly part of a single free market system. There is also evidence that divisions between rich and poor are escalating. We are also witnessing a resurgence of nationalism both within and across national boundaries as different groups seek to regain a dignity and identity which has been denied them. There is increasing concern about the quality of air and water which is shared across continents, and concern that action to counter this is insufficient even after the 1992 Rio Summit. There is an increasing gap between the life experiences of the peoples of the 'North' and of the 'South'. The continuing flow of polluting technologies from the 'North' to the 'South' has become even more significant given the apparent accessibility of nuclear materials. Such social, cultural, environmental, economic and political factors are all operating interdependently within a single global system. They are all issues which relate directly to citizenship and citizenship education. The context is confusing and yet the individual citizen needs to make informed and responsible decisions. Understanding the role of the citizen within this web of activity requires an holistic approach which recognises the connections between these processes and the personal choices and behaviours of the individual. Learning about citizenship requires an interdisciplinary approach which promotes awareness of the relationships between the personal, the political and the global.

Such conceptions of citizenship have been fundamental to the work of many Non-Governmental Organisations (NGOs). There are many well-established NGOs in Britain which include education programmes to encourage participation in their activities. For example, in the last calendar year two handbooks providing guidance for teachers in their work to promote active and responsible citizenship have been produced with support and financial backing from such NGOs. Oxfam, Christian Aid and Rowntree Charitable Foundation have together funded the World Studies Trust and the publication of the teacher's handbook *Learning from Experience* written by Miriam Steiner, National Coordinator of World Studies Project (Steiner, 1994). The World Wide Fund for Nature has similarly funded the practical classroom guide *Educating for the Future* written by David Hicks, Coordinator of the Global Future Project (Hicks, 1994). Both of these texts include a clear definition of aims for the kind of citizenship education which is concerned with promoting active responses and with developing children's understanding of rights and responsibilities.

## Identifying aims for education for citizenship in a changing world

A group of children (Years 3–6) in a school near the centre of Bristol had a problem with the guinea-pigs in their classroom. The guinea-pigs had babies and there were now more guinea-pig mouths to feed. This was expensive and the funds had run out. The children had become more confident about solving this kind of problem during the year because they had been working alongside a small local action group which was creating a city farm on a site where some houses had been demolished. They had visited this developing city farm once a week over a period of a year. They had been partly responsible for the construction of one of the first features of the farm – the duck pond. They had helped lay paths, sow fields of grass for animal pasture and plant a variety of trees. They had learnt about the needs of chickens, goats and sheep and they had begun to learn how to handle them. They had developed a respect for the skills of shepherds and goatherds. They had been part of the development, from scratch, of a new exciting local facility which they visited after school and at the weekends. They had experienced disappointments when some of their work was undone through an unfortunate act of vandalism. They had developed a respect for the managers of the farm and for their commitment to the project.

It was hardly surprising then that the guinea-pig crisis did not represent too big a problem for them. They quickly thought of the idea of making and selling biscuits on a daily basis on the school site. The process involved the children in collaborative planning and implementation for which they had to exercise responsibility. Simple and cheap recipes were identified, costings were done, some research was conducted about possible demands. The cooker was booked for particular times, a fair cooking rota was organised and plans were made for the buying of ingredients, the washing-up of dirty utensils, the distribution of biscuits, the collection of the monies, the identification of surplus and, last but not least, the buying of the guinea-pig foodstuffs.

This all happened some time ago now and the impact of these and other similar experiences on these children may never be known. They were children who had been identified as having moderate learning difficulties. It was gratifying to meet one pupil who during our first conversation for 6 years offered the remark: 'That farm is still there you know'. He was right – it is still there today and must stand in his mind as one of the great achievements of the past.

He is now one of a generation of young people, many of whom are seeking a variety of strategies to ensure that their work as citizens is purposeful, responsible and effective and relates to issues of rights and responsibilities. Many of them have turned their backs on mainstream political activity as a means to change society and have committed themselves to a range of alternative activist programmes. In a recent newspaper article, Vidal (1994) has published some revealing comments by young members of such groups. The quotations below are selected from his article:

*Thomas Harding, 26:* I've never voted. I see no point in it. My enfranchisement doesn't exist but I feel I'm working on many political levels for a better society. I made a series of films about the world's great activists and discovered a common thread – they worked with local people in such a way that before long whole communities were fighting a common cause. And they managed to change things....

*Nick Jukes:* I've started a local exchange trading scheme in Leicester to give people an alternative to the money economy. We stopped a road being pushed through one community and now we are working with the residents to get a permaculture site on former allotments area. We hope to get a community garden. You don't get anything from appealing to government or bureaucratic organisations, but people at the grassroots can run things themselves. People can organise themselves in a co-operative way. The struggle is to create the structures to let co-operation come out.

*Carolyn Lewis, 19:* I am working with the Freedom Network to try to oppose the Criminal Justice Bill...we're based in a derelict dole office.... If I go to Parliament and talk to politicians, I feel they are out of touch. We see hierarchical power structures dominated by men and decisions made without consultation.... Yet there are all sorts of other organisations that we can feel part of and we join them. You feel more empowered.

*Guy Linley-Adams, 27:* I was attracted to pressure groups because they seem to be doing things rather than talking about them. They are forcing the pace of social change.... I work at Friends of the Earth but the environment is not on the party politicians' real agenda; the things which concern me are not valued by party leaders.

*Anita Barton, 22:* I find the young are swapping hats all the time, fighting for each others' causes, making all the links between themselves, between the Third World, and broadening out the debate so it becomes one cause. My generation has been spoon fed individualism and the need to make money. Any fool can see that's only part of the story. (Vidal, 1994)

These comments are all by young citizens who are working for change in their own ways, rather like the city farm project leaders who engaged the interest and enthusiasm of the school children in the last example. They are all concerned to take responsibilities and to work in the cause of social justice. They have all despaired of formal democratic operations although they each expressed a commitment to democratic and human rights principles. Their personal experience has been a foundation for their political actions. They have all displayed a strong sense of social responsibility that, in the case of Anita Barton, extends across national boundaries. Although it would be a matter of regret to encounter such disillusionment with formal political processes in our pupils in schools, as teachers we would nevertheless welcome and want to nurture such imaginative, wholehearted and sensitive responses from them.

A number of sources are accessible to teachers who are seeking to identify a set of aims and to clarify a reflective set of values related to education for active and responsible citizenship. A key text published by the Council of Europe outlines the recommendations of the Committee of Ministers to member states on teaching and learning about human rights in schools (*see* Appendix). It provides reassuring legitimation for teachers who want to promote work in this field but who have perhaps been distracted by the thought that it does not relate precisely to the main requirements of the National Curriculum. A useful discussion of these recommendations is provided in Starkey (1991). Other useful sources for teachers are Steiner (1994) and Hicks (1994).

These texts have much in common in terms of the aims which they identified; an overview of the relevant knowledge, concepts, skills and

---

**Knowledge:** human rights, responsibilities, freedoms, discrimination, culture, democracy, different kinds of future, sustainability

**Concepts:** social change, distribution of power, peace and conflict, interdependence

**Skills:** self-expression, enquiry, handling evidence, communication, understanding differences, establishing positive and non-oppresive relationships, conflict resolution, taking responsibility, participating in decisions

**Classroom ethos/climate:** learning democracy in a democratic classroom, learning about human rights and justice in a school where there is justice and fairness

---

**Figure 6.1** Key components of education for citizenship (Sources: Hicks, 1994; NCC, 1990a,b,c; Rowe and Newton, 1994; Starkey, 1991; Steiner, 1994.)

classroom ethos is presented in Figure 6.1.

The main humanities subjects of geography, history and religious education provide many opportunities for the promotion of these aims.The model for citizenship education outlined in Figure 6.2 provides a summary of the processes described in this chapter. It emphasises the significance of children's own experience and the teacher's role in making links between these experiences and other events in the school, the community and the wider world. A reflexive set of values is provided through consideration of a human rights perspective. A principal concern within this model is the ethos of the classroom and the school.

## Education for active citizenship in and beyond the classroom

In an inner urban school a group of 9- and 10-year-old children had been making contacts with children in another school in the Bristol area. Their own school served a mixed community. A majority of the families were of African Caribbean or Asian

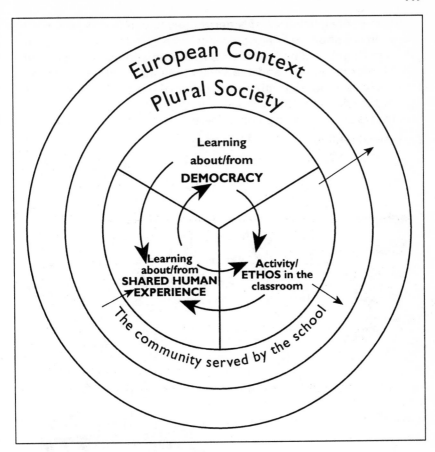

**Figure 6.2** Model for citizenship education

origin. The children had been sharing some of the products of their curriculum work through an exchange of packages sent by post. Each of the teachers had also made a short visit to introduce themselves to the children in the other class. Photographs, Identikit portraits and autobiographical accounts made up some of the first packages, but soon the focus turned to an exchange of information about the local environment of the school. The children did an analysis of places they liked in their school environment, places they did not like and places they would like to change. They shared information about small scale changes that they had effected to improve the environment, including participation in the creation of a garden/pond area.

Their excitement grew stronger when they were offered an opportunity to start a similar communication with children in a school in the Oban area of Nigeria. They had in fact already tried to start an ongoing communication with children in a school in Kibi in Ghana and had taken care to design and make a beautiful batik representing friendship which they included in a package to them (*see* photograph on the cover of the book). They never heard back from this school, but this did not dampen their enthusiasm for making links. There was a long and thoughtful

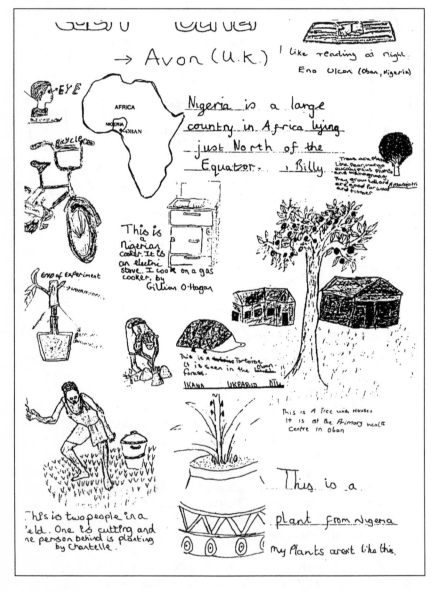

**Figure 6.3** Learning from each other: children in Bristol and Oban, Nigeria

discussion about the resources which the children might have in their school in Nigeria and the children decided that their first communication should be simple, direct and not involve the use of expensive materials. They communicated through drawing and writing about their everyday lives, marking the time of day for each activity on some prepared clock-faces. The package was despatched, but the reply did not come for a long time, not in fact until they had moved into the next year group. But the response was worth waiting for. The information was of immediate interest to the whole class and they used the materials received to make collages as part of a display. An example is shown in Figure 6.3.

Later in the year when the news began to arrive about the people's demolition of the Berlin Wall, the same children approached the headteacher for the names of some schools to write to in East Germany. They had become confident enough to want to communicate with and learn from others in the wider world.

## A story from Prague: on renting a flat for a week

This chapter would perhaps not be complete without some personal account related to being a citizen. The experience is one shared by two of the authors of this book:

In September 1994 we were fortunate to be able to participate in a teacher education conference in Prague and fortunate also to be given the address of B. who was able to find us cheap accommodation in the centre of the city. He met us at the airport and described his job to us as he drove us towards the flat. He is a property surveyor and has been very busy recently mediating disputes over properties which returning Czech nationals are now able to reclaim following the collapse of the Warsaw bloc. In particular he had the job of establishing the precise dimensions of properties, many of which had changed almost beyond recognition since the war years. This seemed a very difficult job for any professional citizen.

We had only been in the flat for 10 minutes when we had our first visitor. We were at first surprised to hear a knock at the door as we did not know anybody in this city apart from B. We were even more surprised when the man at the door asked us how long we had been living there. The answer 'Ten minutes' hardly seemed credible to him. He explained that he had been born in 1922 and had lived with his parents and family in the flat on the opposite side of the corridor. He wanted to know who lived there now. He described how he loved the city of Prague, how he and his family had to endure occupation by the Nazis in the war years and how the arrival of Soviet forces had not brought relief. He described how in desperation he had escaped to Germany in 1949, as it happened the year of our births. He had hated his exile and even now longed to return to live in Prague. He did not conceal his hatred of Germans whose aim, he claimed, was always 'to dominate'. He said they achieved this aim either through politics and military power or through economics. He had only a little time left on this visit and felt he would have to come back in a year's time. He left almost as quickly as he came, leaving us with a sense of bewilderment that citizenship of any country could involve such complexities. There was much to learn about Prague, about the Czech Republic and about Central Europe before we could begin to understand what our own personal involvement would be...and possibly had already been.

## Conclusion

The conclusion of this chapter is that conceptions of citizenship are complex and multilayered. The case studies in this chapter did not relate directly to the formal political sphere as is often characterised by decision making at the level of local and central government. In the case of the bypass, the formal political and legal processes had already been fulfilled and a decision to build the road had been made. In this case the political activities described are a form of direct action by citizens reflecting strongly felt personal beliefs. In the school-based studies the interactions described were at an institutional and inter-personal level. Such a choice of case study is not intended to indicate a disinterest in the formal democratic processes which need to be described and explained to children during their schooling. Rather it has been argued that citizenship and citizenship education has two interconnected dimensions – the political and the personal. Our concern in this chapter has been to demonstrate opportunities for teachers to enable children to use the experience and discussion of their interpersonal and institutional worlds to inform their developing understanding of interactions in the wider political sphere.

The pedagogical implications of this are that it is important to teach children to use the language of citizenship through exploring and reflecting on their own everyday personal experiences. It is important that they begin to recognise that their own actions affect and are affected by actions in the wider world. It is important that they recognise the significance of Human Rights Conventions to the development of values underpinning their own behaviours and the behaviours of others as citizens in society.

# CHAPTER SEVEN

# European Dimensions

It should perhaps not be a surprise that 'the European dimension' remains a considerable enigma within the National Curriculum framework. For the obvious paradox of a European dimension in a national framework may be but a reflection of the disquiet and ambivalence within the present Conservative government (and, it must be said, within British society) about a commitment to Europe. In this chapter we start by considering what concept children have of Europe. We then consider what does actually constitute Europe in the late twentieth century. It is a phenomenon which is changing (as it always has done) more rapidly than ever before.

Having established that European identity is a key aspect of the child's developing sense of self in society, we consider possible ways of approaching European studies within the primary curriculum. In conclusion we look in brief at the approach to humanities in the primary schools of other European countries and we review the joint implications of these last three chapters – what does it mean to have a humanities curriculum which is based on commitments to citizenship, the environment and Europe? In this consideration we again emphasise the necessity of avoiding Eurocentrism and the need for establishing an understanding of international, global interdependence.

## Images of Europe

Children in a primary classroom to the north of Bristol had been undertaking a project on Europe. The evidence of this consisted of a number of displays on wall panels between the classroom windows. At the top of each panel was a painting of a nation's flag and beneath this was a list of facts about the particular country: population, language, climate, landscape, major industries and so on.

These potted geographies do provide a child with a concept of a nation, but they also have considerable drawbacks. First, they emphasise nation states, as opposed to a united Europe. But secondly they lead to a simplistic and stereotypical notion of these nations. They can ignore some of the key elements of the geography of a particular region. For example, the existence of significant minority groups, with their own languages and religions, can easily be overlooked. The inter-relationship between a country and its neighbours is also often ignored.

In 1992–93, Sharonjit Bassi, a fourth year BEd student, was working with children in an east Bristol junior school. She was investigating how they perceived places in the world around them. Her work with six children aged 8 and six children aged 10, involved among other activities:

(a) asking them to list the names of countries which they could recall;and
(b) asking them to draw a map of the world; she was able to encourage them to do this without a feeling of being tested.

Some results of the first activity are shown in Figure 7.1. Here there is some indication of greater knowledge of European than of non-European countries (as well as some confusion between continents and countries). Figure 7.2 presents two of the maps drawn in response to the second activity.

The maps also demonstrate greater knowledge of European countries. In the Year 3 child's picture, the location of Italy, Germany and France on the same landmass as Cornwall and Scotland is particularly interesting. The Year 5 child has made a good representation of the shapes of landmasses and reveals knowledge of specific countries in large continents, for example Argentina in South America and Chad and Somalia in Africa.

From a number of studies into children's knowledge of other countries, reviewed by Wiegand (1992), it emerges that the knowledge of most British children up to the age of 11 is dominated by western Europe. The two 'foreign' countries most known about are France and Spain. It also emerges that the countries of eastern and indeed central Europe are not known about to any great extent. This is surprising given that some of this work was carried out in the 1990s, some time after the collapse of the Berlin Wall and the USSR. Sharonjit Bassi's work reported above, did in fact reveal some awareness of Russia.

Such a finding calls into question the significance of the media in shaping children's perceptions of the world. The dominance of France and Spain perhaps indicates that holiday experiences are most significant – that actual experience does indeed have much greater influence than mediated vicarious experience.

| Countries named by six Year 3 children | | Countries named by six Year 5 children | |
|---|---|---|---|
| **Countries mentioned** | **Number of mentions** | **Countries mentioned** | **Number of mentions** |
| England | 6 | England | 6 |
| America | 6 | France | 6 |
| Wales | 5 | America | 6 |
| Denmark | 5 | Ireland | 5 |
| Sweden | 5 | Wales | 5 |
| France | 5 | Germany | 5 |
| Spain | 5 | Italy | 4 |
| Africa | 5 | Scotland | 3 |
| Ireland | 3 | Denmark | 3 |
| Scotland | 3 | Spain | 3 |
| Australia | 3 | Canada | 3 |
| Canada | 2 | Norway | 2 |
| Brazil | 2 | Sweden | 2 |
| Greece | 1 | Africa | 2 |
| Russia | 1 | Greece | 2 |
| Germany | 1 | Russia | 2 |
| Cyprus | 1 | China | 2 |
| Holland | 1 | Japan | 2 |
| Jamaica | 1 | Australia | 2 |
| India | 1 | Iceland | 2 |
| New Zealand | 1 | Poland | 2 |
| | | Greenland | 2 |
| | | Holland | 2 |
| | | Egypt | 2 |
| | | Finland | 1 |
| | | Portugal | 1 |
| | | Albania | 1 |
| | | Yugoslavia | 1 |
| | | New Zealand | 1 |
| | | Cyprus | 1 |
| | | Brazil | 1 |
| | | Nepal | 1 |
| | | Bolivia | 1 |

**Figure 7.1** Countries mentioned by 7 and 10 year olds (Years 3 and 5, respectively)

However, there is an exception to this pattern in those inner urban primary schools where the children's ethnic origins are much more diverse, and where knowledge of European countries can be less than that of some countries of origin (Figure 7.3). This provides us with a reminder of the dangers of Eurocentrism in the curriculum.

If the media are less influential than might be expected in informing basic knowledge about countries, this does not mean that they do not play a profound part in shaping children's attitudes towards such countries. The influence of stereotypical television sitcoms such as *'Allo 'Allo* or of soaps like the now defunct *Eldorado*, can be seen in children's images of European countries. Even nursery children, few of whom had actually been to Spain, mentioned a beach, hotel, sea, sun and sand (Lambert and Wiegand, 1990; cited by Wiegand, 1992).

## The nature of 'the new Europe'

What is actually meant by 'Europe'? It has always been a complex concept, partly because its landmass is not separated from Asia, but also because of the complexity of history in the region. The current configuration of nation states in the region is only the latest in an almost continually changing scenario. The nation state concept itself is a very European one, a 'modern' and relatively recent creation, and yet the history of Europe demonstrates what a problematic one it is. One only has to consider the First and Second World Wars and to be reminded of the scale of conflict within the former Yugoslavia (as we write), or the 25 years of struggle in the north of Ireland, to recognise the frequent failure of the nation state concept to lead to peaceful and effective co-existence.

In the late twentieth century the two dominant political themes in Europe are the move towards a federation of states on the one hand and, on the other, the re-emergence of independent nations which were, until the current decade, under the influence or direct rule of the Soviet Union. The contemporary paradox of Europe then is that these two tendencies are in tension with each other. On the one hand we see the emergence of a supra-national state, on the other we see the resurgence of Balkanisation, not only in former Yugoslavia, but in the Baltic states and the former Czecho-slovakia, for example. However, it would be mistaken to suggest that these tendencies relate respectively only to the former west and the former east. For in their urgent desire to join the European community, countries such as Hungary, the Czech Republic and the Slovak Republic are demonstrating a desire to federate. And, at the same time, there are nationalist movements in Wales and Scotland, the Basque region and Catalonia, which demonstrate tendencies to subdivide.

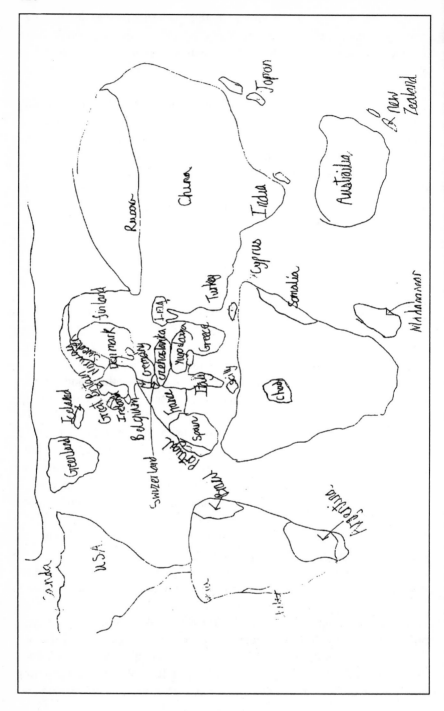

**Figure 7.2 (a)**  A Year 3 child's image of the world.

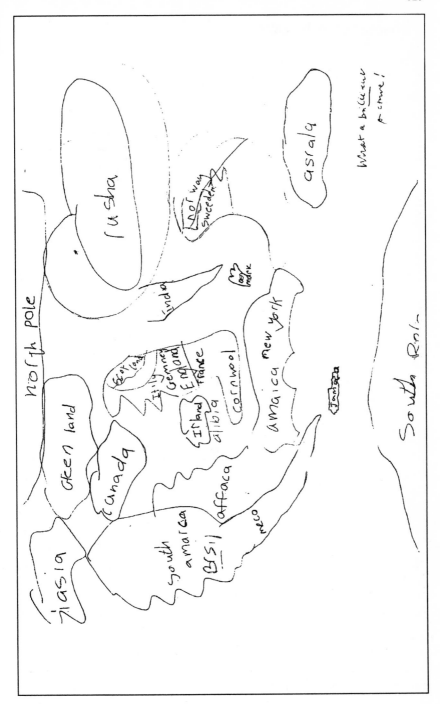

**Figure 7.2 (b)** A Year 5 child's image of the world

130

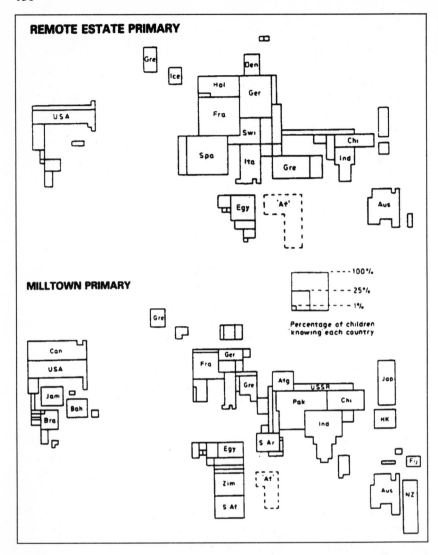

**Figure 7.3** The 'known world' of children from two Yorkshire schools. The area of each country is drawn proportional to the number of children 'knowing it' (Source: Wiegand, 1992: 72–73.)

Contemporary nationalism has at least two facets. The first is the desire for a cultural identity based on traditional language, sometimes religion and other cultural attributes. The second is the nationalism of the superstate, based on economic arrangements and trade agreements which favour the region as a whole.

So it is that these apparently contradictory tendencies lead to a considerable amount of political and social difficulty. Throughout Europe there has recently been a rise of ultra-nationalism and ethnic tension. In Latvia, there is evidence of discrimination being experienced by people of Russian origin, who are sometimes seen as reminders of the former oppressors. In southern Slovakia and in northern Romania (Transylvania) ethnic Hungarians are claiming that they are experiencing systematic discrimination. In the new 'united' Germany, Turkish migrant workers have been murdered and have had their homes destroyed. In France too, the rise of Le Pen's National Front has been associated with intimidatory violence towards African migrants. And of course in Britain, racist attacks on Black and Asian people continue. Throughout Europe, the experience of Gypsies is one of discrimination and abuse.

## The European dimension within the National Curriculum

What can Europe mean to young children? What is clear is that it must be our aim to give children some insight into the complexity and fluidity of Europe, both of which are too often ignored in current practice.

Some of this complexity was revealed by the experience of some student teachers who spent several weeks in Hungary during 1992. Their expectations of Hungarian society had been largely formed by media accounts of 'oppressive communism'. However, they found the society to be a welcoming one and indeed one where many values were similar to those of Britain. In the schools they worked in they found what they felt was a didactic and 'traditional' approach to teaching and learning, but they did not find that it was oppressive for children. They noted a happy atmosphere and good relationships between children and teachers. Overall it was very difficult for them to understand what they found because of the rapid rate of change. But it was not only the changes in Hungary that made this difficult. The students' experience of the reassertion of traditional values in British education and culture sometimes meant they felt the two societies were moving in opposite directions towards the same point but yet would 'pass each other' and their previous relationship would be reversed.

The National Curriculum for England provides limited guidance on appropriate study of Europe. The history curriculum of 1988 included a unit called Invaders and Settlers, which could include consideration of migration from mainland Europe into Britain. The history of Ancient Greece also featured and this provided an opportunity to study European elements in the cultural inheritance of Britain. In the post-Dearing curriculum we find that there is a greater emphasis on 'British history', with immigration and emigration no longer being mentioned explicitly. In

Key Stage 1 children are required to study British history, in Key Stage 2 six out of eight Units must be British; it is only at Key Stage 3, in the secondary school that children have to study elements of European history. However, it is possible to be imaginative as a teacher in how the units are actually taught, and it may well be that an interpretation of 'British' which emphasises British regional (i.e. European) and global relations can be pursued (*see* Pankhania, 1994).

With regards to geography, the 1988 initial proposals included 'the UK within the European Community' as an attainment target in its own right. In the curriculum adopted in 1988–89 this became subsumed in attainment target 2, 'knowledge and understanding of places' and children in the primary school were not required to study a European locality unless they were working at level 5, the highest 'normal' level in the primary school. In the post-Dearing geography curriculum, in something of a contrast with the history orders, children in Key Stage 1 are required to develop an awareness of a wider world than the United Kingdom.

We have referred in the previous two chapters to National Curriculum Council guidance on, respectively, environmental education and citizenship education. These two topics were designated as cross-curricular themes. The European dimension is, on the other hand, designated a cross-curricular dimension, along with multicultural education (*see* NCC, 1990a). As with multicultural education, neither the NCC nor SCAA, its successor, have as yet seen fit to produce guidance on this topic, although the Department for Education did produce a pack for schools entitled *The European Dimension* in 1992. Given the way in which all cross-curricular elements have been played down since the realisation of the vast overload in the National Curriculum, it is perhaps unwise to make too much of this omission by NCC/SCAA. However, the fact remains that this is very much an area for teachers' professional judgement and there is considerable scope for school-based curriculum development. Such an approach was indeed taken in the 'Teaching about Europe in the primary school' project co-ordinated by Gordon Bell (Bell, 1991).

Within teacher education there has been some recognition of the European dimension. Indeed the criteria for course accreditation established by the Secretary of State in 1989 included a stipulation that courses should include a European element. Given the overload of the teacher education curriculum, this has rarely led to more than superficial treatment. The fact that school experience (teaching practice) in any non-British setting was not deemed to 'count' for accreditation purposes has meant that even exchange visits to European primary schools have not developed in teacher education to the extent that they might have. It is only in institutions such as our own, where the amount of school experience within the course has greatly exceeded the minimum requirement laid down in government regulations, that significant amounts of time have been spent in European countries. Using European Community funding (particularly the ERASMUS and TEMPUS programmes) students have been able to gain experience of schools in Denmark, Holland, Hungary or Latvia. Plans are afoot to offer opportunities in Greece, Portugal, Spain and elsewhere.

It is difficult to judge the effect of the 'reforms' in teacher education which are being implemented at the time of writing. The removal of content criteria creates more flexibility for course design, but the increase in school experience time means that it will be more difficult for students to undertake exchanges unless the time in European schools can be counted, which would seem to be highly sensible. The difficulties of fitting any European experience into the one-year PGCE course will remain, and indeed may be mirrored on the 3-year-six subject BEd course which the government is encouraging institutions to adopt.

The developments in teacher education were in part a response to initiatives stemming from the Council of Europe itself. A 1988 statement by the ministers of education called for a strengthening in young people of a sense of European identity, for them to be prepared to take part in the economic and social development of the Community and to improve their knowledge of the Community and its member states (*see* Bell, 1991, for a full account of these aspects).

The UK government's difficulty over the Maastricht Treaty and its opting out from the social chapter are additional evidence of the apparently less than total commitment to the European dimension within education.

## Work with children

Bell (1991:60) lists a variety of approaches and starting points for teaching and learning about Europe. These include:

- a single country study
- a European theme
- an inter-cultural approach
- a subject-based framework.

Earlier in this chapter we implicitly criticised an approach to the curriculum based on profiles of nation states. While the history and geography of current nations are important content areas and children will need to develop their knowledge of these, nevertheless we believe it is more important at this stage that children develop an understanding of the nature of Europe as a whole and of similarities and differences amongst its peoples. Such an approach indicates that a European awareness should imbue much of the work which children do. When they are studying particular topics or themes, whichever subject or subjects are being dealt with, the wider context of Europe should be considered. So, for example, in one primary school where 8- and 9-year-old children were studying printing and newspapers, much interest was shown in looking at papers published in a variety of European countries and comparing the news which they included – both the world news and the national news.

Themes which are particularly pertinent to the questions of Europe would include studies of migration, transport, water and air pollution, languages and borders. One interesting resource pack developed in Switzerland on the subject of borders was designed to help children understand both the significance and the arbitrariness of borders. Children undertake various role play and simulation activities which enable them to explore the political and social implications of frontiers.

A second major element in the effective study of matters European is the establishment of direct contact with people in other European locations. Many LEAs have established European offices, one purpose of which is to stimulate exchange and communication between teachers, pupils and schools around Europe. Given that modern European languages do not feature in the curriculum of British primary schools, a difficulty can be posed for effective communication. However, many children of the same age in other European countries do study English and so progress can be made. Primary schools may also organise links on the back of links established by their local secondary school.

Such links can take many different forms, ranging from communication by letter, through exchange of pictures, photographs and through fax or e-mail, to full-scale exchange programmes. The latter would tend only to involve the oldest primary children, and can be very expensive and therefore unavailable to some families. One primary school near Bristol organised a 3–4 day visit for its Year 6 children to Paris.

In another school (referred to in Chapter 6; *see* pages 110–111) a discussion about the school curriculum with senior staff revealed that they would like to see the development of a global dimension so that their children would be made more aware of their connections with the wider world. They recalled the success of an earlier 'curriculum linking' project which supported communications between children across different classrooms in Europe. It was recognised that this work had excited the children and had provided opportunities for them to have some experience of cultural differences. Previous links had been with children in schools in EC countries, though staff were expressing an interest in making links with schools in Central Europe. One staff member commented that:

> this may provide more opportunities for the children to explore differences as well as similarities in lifestyles and material conditions.

This is a school which has already had experience of hosting a group of children from a school in Hungary. This was in part facilitated by a Hungarian education student who had worked in the school during a mobility programme funded by TEMPUS (*see* above).

Resources are a matter for careful consideration. There is no shortage of texts, videos and charts, particularly about western Europe. However, there is a shortage of available material covering eastern Europe, and there is a general problem which affects all European resource material. This is the problem of continual change. Teachers must have accurate and up-to-date material. This may often lead to the use of press material alongside textbooks. Coverage in the press of European news has improved quite rapidly over recent years (especially in *The Guardian*; *The European* is also very useful).

## European primary schools

In most other countries within Europe, humanities is less visible than many other subjects as a field of study, particularly in the primary school. Nevertheless most curricula do include an element which relates to citizenship or perhaps 'civics'. Similarly most curricula include elements of history and geography, relating mainly to the particular nation concerned. A European dimension may well appear, although often in a highly selective form, notably associated with language teaching. Thus, for example, we have observed 9- and 10-year-old Hungarian children being taught about aspects of British culture and history in English language classes.

With some local exceptions, the notion of multicultural or intercultural education is less well developed in other European countries although in many places considerable attention is given to the teaching and learning of children's first language when it is not the national language. This is in line with Article 48 of the Treaty of Rome (1977; *see* Tulasiewicz, 1993).

In countries which were formerly associated with the Soviet Union, before its demise, there was an element in the curriculum designed to encourage good citizenship. That this appeared to be of a more directly ideological nature than its equivalent in the capitalist societies, is possibly a view which reflects the relative invisibility of western ideologies rather than anything else. Indeed a critique of the English National Curriculum as a whole can be developed which demonstrates that it includes profoundly nationalistic ideological elements (*see* King and Reiss, 1993; or Hardy and Vieler-Porter, 1990). Furthermore, if we examine the school curriculum in France, we in fact find that at least 1 hour per week is spent on civic education in both primary and secondary schools. Hugh Starkey in his valuable comparison of English and French approaches to citizenship, quotes from the official French text:

> Having an essentially moral dimension, civic education should encourage honesty, courage, the rejection of racism in all its forms, love of the Republic. (Starkey, 1992:87)

If being European means anything and if education has a legitimate role in helping young people to become European, then children must both be given knowledge about Europe and be enabled to develop a critical understanding of the complex notion of citizenship. Referring to a view expressed at a British Council seminar in 1990, Tulasiewicz (1993:242) suggests that:

> The distinction made...between preparing a European Citizen and teaching about Europe is not helpful, since a citizen must be knowledgeable about things European to acquire the right attitudes and dispositions.

We referred to the problem of acquiring accurate resources in Britain. This is a problem throughout Europe. In particular there is felt to be a great need to rewrite texts about national and European history in a number of the recently 'liberated' countries of eastern and central Europe. This is a complex task. Experience which some of us have had of working in Latvia has made us very aware of the delicacy of portraying a national culture in school texts in a positive but non-xenophobic way and of portraying a history of subordination (Latvia was part of the USSR from 1940 until 1991) in an honest and accurate way which does not undermine the rights of significant minorities within the community.

## European environmental citizenship?

One of the main purposes in devoting such space to consideration to the study of Europe is that we believe that through a study of Europe, children's understanding of the whole world can be significantly enhanced. The interdependence of peoples, nations, economies and cultures in the European context, is mirrored in global interdependence.

Through examining people, processes and patterns within Europe, children can start to understand people, process and patterns across the world and start to understand the relationship of Europe to other global regions, whether they be economic blocs or physical masses.

In his book on the European dimension in primary schools, Bell makes a similar point, insisting that the European dimension is but one facet of promoting education for international understanding (Figure 7.4).

For our part, in the current text we would wish to emphasise the importance of the themes of the last three chapters and to draw attention to the inter-connections between these three themes, particularly looking ahead to education in our schools in the twenty first century (Figure 7.5).

As the three last chapters have shown, there is enormous overlap between these three concerns. One is unlikely to act in a way which aims to sustain the environment without being aware of the responsibilities of citizenship. Europe itself is a physical and social environment which has

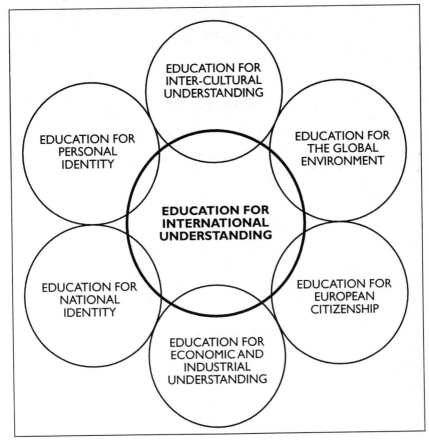

**Figure 7.4** Developing a European dimension (Source: Bell, 1991:65)

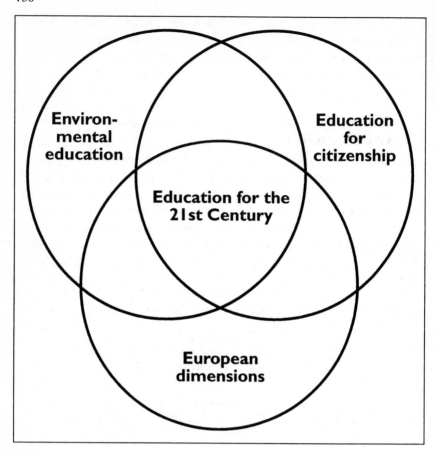

**Figure 7.5** Education for the twenty-first century

a shared but varied history. A river which rises in one country may carry minerals or pollutants into another. The new Europe is one in which a vast number of people live, whose rights are affected not only by the country which they live in, but often by their origins whether they be within Europe or elsewhere. We can in a meaningful way suggest that part of our goal is to provide an education for European environmental citizenship.

The danger of any such proposition is that we forget that each of these elements is continually changing. The environment, citizenship and Europe may seem like rather different, albeit overlapping categories, but ongoing change and redefinition is one thing they have in common. That is one reason why it is so important that teachers are given the opportunity and support to exercise their professionalism through adapting and developing the curriculum.

# CHAPTER EIGHT

# *Staged Events and Experiential Learning*

The aim of this chapter is to draw upon earlier chapters to clarify ideas about some effective approaches to humanities teaching. In particular, it will be argued that experiential learning and cross-curricular approaches to learning are a particularly effective way of developing understanding in the humanities. In this chapter we shall emphasise the importance of empathy in helping children to decentre and to take on board differing viewpoints. With this in mind we shall include a discussion of the value of the more elaborate 'staged event' along with the use of role play and drama in the learning of history in everyday classroom contexts. We will show how opportunities can be made for promoting the learning of religious education and geography as well as for exploring questions of human experience in general such as conflict resolution.

## The mental switch from present to past

Nearly 50 years ago now, the *Beano* comic used to feature the adventures of a schoolboy called Jimmy, whose shorts had been patched with a piece of magic carpet. This unusual feature of his attire enabled Jimmy to be transported back in time and to find himself participating in one or another historical event. 'Jimmy and his magic patch' became a useful device for the reader to be instantaneously whisked from the present-day world to a period in the past. Since the days of H.G. Wells the idea of a time machine has taken on a variety of forms. A more recent example of a time machine which has enthralled more than one generation of school-children is the television series *Dr Who*. Here it is a police telephone kiosk that facilitates the journey back through time. In the context of history taught in schools, one school history coordinator in a Bristol primary school during 1991-92 encouraged all her colleagues in the school to study a history topic with their classes during the same term. Each classroom was transformed into a particular period of history. Visitors to the school encountered a large computer-like time machine, which alerted them to the fact that they were to be transported back in time to a variety of periods in the past. The use of a microprocessor to fulfil the role of a time machine is described below (*see* page 159).

## Through a time tunnel to Anglo-Saxon England

A group of student teachers at the University of the West of England who were preparing a staged event based on Anglo-Saxon England were concerned to find a way of transporting their children back in time. They hit on the idea of making a time tunnel. As the children were ushered into a dimly-lit passage, they passed a series of signs indicating past years and past centuries. A chorus of pre-recorded voices informed them 'You are entering into a time tunnel…'. The children emerged at the far end into a gloomy, damp and spacious cellar area of a mid-eighteenth century building, previously used for storage, but now converted to an early English monastery! From many of the accounts that the children wrote after their visit, it is clear that the process of transportation back in time had made a profound impression. One 8-year-old girl wrote:

> I enjoyed the time tunnel. I thought it was very imaginative. I didn't think grown-ups had so much imagination.

Once children have been spirited to another period of time, conditions are ripe for experiential learning and for becoming involved empathetically in activities associated with other times, places and cultures. In this case, opportunities were provided for the children to imagine what it was like to live in Anglo-Saxon England and to experience, among other things, writing in a Runic script with a quill pen and taking part in the burial of an Anglian monarch.

One boy commented afterwards:

> I learnt that when they had to write that it must have been hard…

and another child wrote:

> I've learnt a lot of things like how to use the feather pens, and how they did their funerals when they placed their shields and helmet in the boat.

# Children and empathy

In providing such opportunities for children to 'go back' into the past and to play as it were in role, it is important to ask whether they can ever provide a complete experience of what it was like to be there at the time. Inevitably, attempts at empathising with people in other places who have long since disappeared will be limited. Furthermore, our interpretations will be distorted by the twentieth century lenses through which we perceive and interpret the past.

What we can do in our attempt to place ourselves in the shoes of those who lived in earlier times, is to take on those human experiences which are as relevant as ever to our late twentieth century world. If our interest is primarily in studying history, the universality of human experience whether now or in earlier times can assist our understanding.

## Understanding other cultures

Sometimes that universal human link can be used to help children understand modern-day issues through their study of the past. One of the authors was interested in devising classroom strategies which would help children to appreciate different cultural perspectives in today's multicultural society. He devised a limited form of staged event set in Roman Britain at a time soon after the Claudian conquest. His class of juniors, in fact the same class that worked on the donkey story (*see* Chapter 4), was firstly divided into two halves with some chosen to act as Romans, the rest as Britons. An imaginary scenario was presented which involved a decision by the Roman authorities to build a road through a particular area of the country. The class was asked to consider a variety of arguments for and against the building of the road. They were then asked to consider all the arguments in two separate 'camps' before joining in a vigorous debate with each other as to whether or not the road should go ahead. The final stage of this activity involved an attempt to resolve the conflict between the two groups in which the whole class considered possible solutions to the dilemma. Here were some of the solutions put forward by the class:

> The Romans give the Britons food, money and clothes. The Britons might then agree to the road.
> The Romans dam the river so that no boats can travel along it any more. Then the Britons decide that they want a road to travel along.
> The Britons could pretend to agree to the road. Later on they could smash the road up.
> The Romans could sneakily build the road during the meeting.

The Britons could use earplugs so that they are not disturbed by noises from the road.
The Britons could poison the Romans' food or water supply. They would feel sick and decide to go home.
The Romans build a wall down either side of the road that they want to build. They then build the road inside these walls.

In their proposals for retrospectively resolving an ancient conflict between two different cultural groups, these children offered solutions which were frequently enterprising and well thought-out. Occasionally their suggestions were as bizarre as they were entertaining, but they were all involved in empathising with the situation and were committed to grappling with issues that have continuing relevance to environmental and citizenship education today.

## Understanding historical concepts

Small-scale staged events involving role play can be regularly used in the classroom to tackle particular historical concepts, especially those which are difficult to explain using a didactic approach.

The National Curriculum Orders for history, following the Dearing review, stress the importance of understanding a number of specified concepts. In organising and communicating their knowledge and understanding of history at Key Stage 2, pupils should be taught:

> The terms necessary to describe the periods and topics studied, including court, monarch, parliament, nation, civilisations, invasion, conquest, settlement, conversion, slavery, trade, industry, law…'. (DFE, 1995)

A good example of a staged event used as an effective way of teaching historical concepts was that used by Estelle Loft. Estelle gave her pupils a limited taste of what it was like to be invaded by the Roman army by simulating an 'invasion' in her classroom. At playtime, Estelle called back a small number of her children whom she cast as 'Romans' and immediately invited them to put on sheets to represent togas. She then did the same herself. When the rest of the class returned from play, they were summarily informed that the Romans had invaded their classroom and had taken control. From now on they would have to do as they were told! In this way, Estelle was able to plunge her class into an empathetic role in which children were forced to take sides and to explore some of the issues which arise in such a situation.

Another different but equally dramatic way of tackling the same concept, on this occasion the end of Roman Britain and the arrival of invaders from the continent of Europe, was developed by one of the authors with a Year 3 class.

One wall of the classroom was made to represent, as realistically as possible, the inside wall of a Romano-British villa in the mid-fourth century AD. The villa was intended to be close to the Bristol Channel. Children studied pictures of Roman wall paintings and reproduced Roman frescoes using poster paints and marbling inks. They then created three window openings in the 'wall' of the villa. Through each of the openings paintings were made to represent long ships of invaders being rowed up the River Severn.

To make the concept of invasion as memorable as possible, the teacher told the class a story based upon evidence from the Roman writer Ammianus Marcellinus who refers to attacks on Britain in AD 367 by Scots and Picts and to the parallel activities of the Franks and Saxons in the English Channel. He also used local evidence from archaeological excavations for the violent destruction of two villas in the Bristol area to suggest what might have happened to this particular villa when the seaborne invaders came onto the land. In fact one of the excavated villas yielded evidence of fire and destruction with human bodies thrown down a well.

All these examples of staged events described above have been drawn from the Romano-British period and have been used by primary teachers to teach elements of what is now the 'Romans, Anglo-Saxons and Vikings in Britain' topic. All provide opportunities for exploring the concept of 'invasion' and also 'conquest' as well as having strong links with 'settlement'.

*Dealing with contemporary situations*

As the first 'Invaders and settlers' example illustrated, staged events can often be used with good effect to help children empathise with present-day human situations around the world.

The possibilities can further be illustrated by referring to a more elaborate form of staged event involving one or more schools working in collaboration. Two of the authors previously working as primary school teachers in two neighbouring inner city primary schools in Bristol, decided to involve their two schools in a collaborative venture entitled 'Kwaku Ananse and the shrinking banknote' in which children were introduced to many geographical and cultural concepts relevant to modern-day developments in other countries in the post-colonial era.

Central to the whole programme were stories about Kwaku Ananse, introduced by a Ghanaian story-teller and interpreted by the children through movement, drama and music by the children. In an early episode, children were encouraged to empathise with a traditional story about Kwaku Ananse in which the hero collects all the wisdom of the world into a pot. Wishing to keep it to himself, he begins to take it to the top of a tall forest tree. Those below call his climbing skills into question. Kwaku loses his temper and drops the pot. Everyone runs around picking up what wisdom they can find in unequal amounts.

The programme also offered pupils plenty of scope for exploring geographical features of Ghana, its economy and its relationship with other more financially affluent countries in the world. In one episode, Kwaku was revealed in his role as a farmer, seeking with the help of friends to grow a succession of crops – yams, maize and cassava – on his land but with little success. It transpired that the chief had given him some poor farm land. Together with his friends, Kwaku searched for some of the wisdom that he had earlier dropped and they discovered bauxite, a material that can be turned into aluminium.

Later episodes in the story centred on how Kwaku became involved in mining bauxite on his land, building an aluminium smelter and damming the river to provide the necessary electric power, with all the inevitable environmental consequences. Ultimately Kwaku became involved and inextricably bound up with a rich American company directed by Mr Smelter. Kwaku's project turned out to be more expensive than he bargained for. Although he had received a cheque for 100 million dollars from multinational companies by way of a capital loan to aid the development, Kwaku quickly accumulated enormous additional expenditure: the cost of rehousing villagers displaced by the dam, hospitals to cater for victims of water-borne diseases and compensation for fisherman downstream from the plant. Kwaku paid each of these bills by tearing a piece off his enormous 100 million dollar banknote. He was left with insufficient money to enable him to excavate his bauxite or to build his factory. (Hence the title of the whole project: 'Kwaku Ananse and the shrinking banknote'.) Mr Smelter was not able to lend him any more money, but the contract with the multinational company was binding. In the end Kwaku was forced to abandon his ambitions and to earn money as an electricity meter reader. Mr Smelter then took over the plant for smelting bauxite which he imported from Alaska.

The children's comments show how well the children grasped the essentials of this real-life situation:

Practically everything was unfair because Mr Smelter won. Ananse got all the blame, but Mr Smelter had ruined him. Also Ananse got a really bad deal – he won some dud land. He deserved some of it – he was always trying to get rich. He deserved what he got in the end.

I liked the moral of the story at the end – it said when you catch wisdom hold onto it because wisdom is slippery -its sort of hang onto what you get. I didn't like that end bit because Mr Smelter hung on to what he got and he got some more.

## The history and empathy debate

We should first consider an aspect of history teaching which has in recent years publicly come under fire, namely the encouragement given by teachers to their pupils to engage in empathy. Many external changes have affected the teaching of history both at primary and secondary school since the days when John Fines and Ray Verrier (Fines and Verrier, 1974) were blazing a trail for drama and role play in schools aimed at enabling pupils to 'get inside' a past period of time. Since that time, however, such devices for developing empathy in pupils have now become established as part of the history teacher's 'stock-in-trade', both at primary and secondary school level. The Schools Council History Project, under the leadership of David Sylvester in the 1970s, gave some prominence to the importance of empathy in the learning of history between the ages of 13 and 16.

This project argued for 'imagination disciplined by evidence', using role-play, simulation games, dramatic reconstructions and debates as well as written and oral reconstructions. The historian has to:

> be able to enter into the mind and feelings of all the persons involved in an event and appreciate their differing attitudes without necessarily approving of their motives. (Schools Council History 13–16 Project, 1976)

What one might call an 'empathy element' has, in recent years, become an established part of the history GCSE syllabus of some examination boards. Questions are posed for both course-work and examinations which invite the students to place themselves in the shoes of a particular person or group of people at a particular point in time.

At primary school level there have been a number of initiatives which have fostered this development. Wood (1982) used role play to generate a spirit of enquiry in young children:

> The class, therefore, come as close as possible to living an historical event.
> This gives the role plays an immediacy and relevance while generating
> excitement and involvement in the class. Pupils are no longer passive
> receptors of facts but active participants and will find role plays a painless
> way to learn.

However, over the past few years, this aspect of history teaching has been singled out for polemical attack by members of the 'new Right' and by some politicians. Indeed, a former prime minister has recently joined those who decry the use of empathy in the learning of history:

> No amount of imaginative sympathy for historical characters or situations can substitute for the initially tedious but ultimately rewarding business of memorising what actually happened. (Thatcher, 1993: 595)

Such a comment not only shows little understanding of what historical study is all about (can one ever know what **actually** happened?) but shows little concern for the reality of how young children learn.

Use of the word 'empathy' has been carefully avoided in documents issued by the National Curriculum Council and SCAA and yet the use of what one might call 'empathetic' approaches is nowadays widespread in primary schools, where they are seen as crucial to helping children to engage in historical study. Knight (1993) who prefers the term 'understanding others', and Cooper (1992) both argue, on the basis of their research, for the inclusion of 'structured dilemmas, role-taking exercises, drama, reason-seeking, shifting patterns of group work, and teaching for "thoughtfulness"' as effective ways of enhancing children's understanding of people in the past, and also in the present (Knight, 1993).

In teaching the humanities at any level, promoting a degree of empathy in young children must be seen as crucial to the development of international and intercultural understanding in the world of today in which they will before long be playing their full part as citizens both in their own communities and of the wider world.

When it comes to achieving higher levels of understanding in relation to history, the argument for using drama and role play is incontrovertible. Goalen and Hendy (1994) have recently convincingly demonstrated that the use of drama at Key Stage 2 can bring high levels of conceptual understanding within a broader band of ability than would have been the case if more traditional approaches had been used.

## Using Ancient Egypt as a focus

The rationale for staged history events which are regularly used at the University of the West of England, as part of the teacher training process, have a number of strands.

First, students have the opportunity to work as historians at their own level, using evidence and working with secondary as well as primary sources to build up a picture of one or more topics within the period chosen.

Second, students have an opportunity to develop their subject knowledge with a view to building up their confidence as future teachers of history. It is expected that some consideration will be given to the place of their chosen topic(s) within a wider conceptual framework, including some attention to chronological and geographical dimensions and the potential for cross-curricular learning.

Third, there is a rich opportunity for students to develop expertise in the application of their subject specialism in a primary-school context. Working with children in a generous teacher–pupil ratio, enables them to focus on the learning process with a small number of children at a time and gives them the opportunity to reflect upon how these children learn.

Fourth, students are able to work collaboratively with one or more fellow students in the planning and implementation as well as with the eventual evaluation of their teaching activities.

Fifth, there is the opportunity for role play and drama as part of the process of learning history. Sometimes, students will themselves use a short piece of drama, possibly in the form of a puppet theatre, to present particular concepts, but more often than not, they will devise role play in an attempt to promote a degree of empathetic understanding of particular aspects of the period in question.

The chosen topic for the 1994 summer event was Ancient Egypt, originally one of the supplementary topics illustrating a past non-European society and now included under Study Unit 6.

The children taking part in this event were from Romney Avenue Junior School, which had originally been built in the 1950s to serve a small local authority housing estate in North Bristol. A mixed-ability class of 22 Year 5 children was combined with 12 other children identified as having special educational needs.

The children had not yet studied Ancient Egypt in school. To establish the children's existing state of knowledge about the Ancient Egyptians, and indeed Egypt, the Year 5 children were given a concept mapping exercise. The children were presented with a blank sheet of paper and asked to identify any things that they already knew about the Ancient Egyptians.

Most children eventually managed to record either in words or in pictures at least some information. There turned out to be a considerable amount of collective knowledge. Having said that, it was clear that the distribution of that knowledge was spread very unevenly among the children. Three girls provided significantly more information than their peers, whilst a number of children could manage little more than the drawing of a pyramid. One of the three girls fluently began her writing:

When somebody says Egypt to me, I think of sand and periomids and the hot air with parm trees....

Another of these girls wrote out a list of 11 facts she could recall about the Egyptians. However, many children found it easier to make drawings, keeping their written information to a minimum. An analysis of the children's responses based on the information is shown in Figure 8.1. This again illustrates the potential for cross-curricular learning in what appears to be an activity based on a single subject area.

| Geographical concepts | | History/R.E. | | History | |
|---|---|---|---|---|---|
| Sun | 6 | Pyramids | 17 | Different costumes | 4 |
| Dry | 1 | Bury dead in tombs | 3 | Papyrus | 2 |
| Hot | 1 | Afterlife | 1 | Picture | 1 |
| Desert | 1 | Brightly coloured | | Jewellery | 1 |
| Mountains | 3 | cases | 1 | Cleopatra | 1 |
| River (Nile) | 4 | Mummies | 5 | Tutankhamen | 1 |
| Red Sea | 3 | Wrapped dead in | | Lord Carnarvon | 3 |
| Sand | 6 | bandages/clothes | 4 | | |
| Palm Trees | 5 | Cat God | 1 | | |
| Camels | 3 | Sun God | 1 | | |
| | | Kill animals for gods | 1 | | |
| | | Dancing | 1 | | |
| | | Big stone statues | 1 | | |

**Figure 8.1** Analysis of children's responses to work on the Egyptians

The whole group was then divided into six groups of mixed ability before coming to the Faculty by coach. Initial brainstorming by the students identified a multiplicity of primary and secondary sources and many ideas for tackling this particular topic with children. The format eventually established for the day was similar to that adopted on other occasions. A plenary introduction was to be followed by a circus of six different sets of activities. The finale was again to be a series of activities led by the student teachers but involving the children. A central permeating issue in the Faculty's courses is equal opportunities. The suggestion that a female Pharoah should play a central role was given added strength by the timely appearance of an article in *History Today* on the subject of Queen Hatshepsut who ruled Egypt for some 18 years with full pharaonic powers during the fifteenth century BC. As one student wrote later, they had provided for the children 'a female Ancient Egyptian role model, which may have challenged their views about gender roles in the ancient world'. This provided an opportunity to study a highly organised society and its considerable achievements which flourished on the African continent long before the British and European societies that the children will have been studying in the rest of their history programmes of study.

## Empathy and Ancient Egypt

On their arrival at the Faculty, the children were straightaway invited to empathise with the Ancient Egyptians by being sent back to the time of Hatshepsut's funeral. They were ushered into a darkened room equipped with three slide projectors, an overhead projector (OHP) and a public address system. They sat on the floor facing a wall which had been adorned among other things with palm trees and pyramids in silhouette. A disembodied voice represented Hatshepsut who had recently died and was awaiting her trial by the gods to assess her fitness to pass to the afterlife. The voice coming over the public address system provided a commentary for a sequence of visual images projected onto the wall: scenes of the Nile and Egyptian landscape and its surviving monuments. The OHP projected a head of Hatshepsut herself onto the wall.

The first task was to locate the event in space and time:

It is very hot and dry and much of the land is mountainous desert. But by the banks of the Nile...the land is fertile and good for farming. The River Nile is very important to our kingdom. It provides us with a plentiful supply of fish and wild birds for food and is a source of precious water for drinking and washing. It is also the main route through Egypt and many boats sail along it, but you must be wary when travelling – there are many crocodiles.

This geographical introduction was followed by an explanation of the historical context. Students had been at pains to get across the enormous stretch of time during which the independent kingdom of ancient Egypt flourished.

Egypt is already an ancient civilization. It is over 1500 years since the first pyramids were built in the 3rd Dynasty.

Having set the scene in general terms, the audience was then given an explanation of who the speaker was:

My name is Hatshepsut. I am a great Pharoah.... Now I have died and I am awaiting my trial by the Gods to allow me to pass into the afterlife. You are seated in my temple at Deir el Bahri....

I have proved myself a powerful and clever ruler, the equal of any man. I even wore a false beard that the Pharoahs wore, as a sign that I was no different to them. I achieved a great deal in my lifetime....

The introduction concluded with this invitation to all the children to await the outcome of Hatshepsut's judgement and to prepare for and participate in her funeral.

I am awaiting my judgement by the Gods.... Go and help prepare some of the treasures I will take to my tomb with me.

The weighing of Hatshepsut's heart against the weight of a feather provided the focal interest for the finale at the end of the morning. This was a dramatic presentation with a number of the student teachers taking part in the roles of the Egyptian deities Anubis, Osiris, Horus and Thoth. The successful balancing of the scales signalled not only Hatshepsut's journey to the afterlife but the beginning of a funerary procession and feast. The students and children were now joined by a group of Year 2 students who had composed a simple piece of processional music using trumpets and percussion.

*Resourcing the Ancient Egyptian event*

The use of primary sources both by the student teachers and by the children was central to the event. As part of the initial preparation students had visited the Egyptian collections in the British Museum and in Bristol City Museum. A large collection of children's books and adult reference works was assembled for the initial brainstorming session. Students also had access to a representative selection of coloured transparencies illustrating Ancient Egypt and to some modern examples of papyrus.

To facilitate the transition from plenary session to group activities the children had been allocated in advance of the visit to one of six groups. Each group of children was assigned a name appropriate to the topic: pyramid, palm tree, snake, the River Nile. On arrival at the Faculty, each was given an Egyptian name written out on a badge which could then have a sign representing their group added to it. The students had discovered that Ancient Egyptian names could be 'unisex', with males and females being distinguished from one another by the use of a symbol after their name.

The circus of activities then followed:

- *Jewellery making (Figure 8.2)* – Studying photographs of original artefacts observed in the British Museum – making necklaces and rings. **Outcome**: all children made a ring and necklace.

- *Wall painting* – Exploring the picture of Nebamun hunting and its significance – looking at evidence for Egyptian paints – painting a large scale outline of the Nebamun hunting scene which had been transferred to a composite sheet of wallpaper.

**Outcome:** the picture was almost completed by the time the final group had taken its turn.

● *Making death masks* – A basic shape of a death mask was provided and the children's task was to decorate it using paint or collage.
**Outcome:** all the children completed a death mask.

● *Playing senet* – The students had developed their own version of the Ancient Egyptian board game known as senet. Evidence for the game has been found in Egyptian tombs.
**Outcome:** all children played the game. Great excitement was generated at times.

● *Making papyrus* – Children were shown the techniques of transforming the papyrus reed into writing material. In addition to being shown examples of papyrus brought from Egypt, a simulated technique was developed using reeds from the Somerset levels. Children were shown the technique of laying fibres both horizontally and vertically to produce a writing surface.

● *Hieroglyphs* – Children had the opportunity to explore several activities which involved them in working with hieroglyphs. They had opportunities to decipher hieroglyphs which were incorporated into a simple board game. Children also had the opportunity to use hieroglyphs to spell out their Egyptian names and to write on the simulated papyrus.

*Reflecting on the Egyptian event*

We now return to the rationale for events of this kind. At this point it will be appropriate to let the student teachers speak for themselves:

*Lyn:* ...it was essential that I developed my knowledge to make the day a success. I also enjoyed the research aspect involved in the topic. I knew very little about the subject, then I went off and researched and now feel more confident with Egypt.

This student also felt that the opportunities for planning such an event had shown her not to be too ambitious in planning. There was also valuable experience of how to use brainstorming and museum visits for generating ideas.

*Barbara:* ...I found that the prospect of having to produce an Egyptian day provided an incentive for my learning. I felt that I was learning for a real purpose and that the success of the end product depended on the amount of research and effort I was prepared to make.

152

**Figure 8.2** Ancient Egypt event: children making jewellery

Despite the Faculty's commitment to equal opportunities, and the choice of a female Pharoah as the central character for this Egyptian event, the realities of life within one of the collaborative student groups followed a stereotypical pattern. These students (a mixed group of female and male mature students) themselves reflected upon what had taken place in their group planning at a later stage. They had assumed from the outset that the men in the group would take charge of the PA equipment and slide projectors. It was the female members of the group and they alone who took the initiative to distribute drinks and fruit to the children during the funeral feast. The students later realised what had happened and resolved that next time they would do things differently!

It would be a useful means of assessing pupils' learning to invite them following an intensive period of study to repeat the concept mapping exercise which was undertaken before their visit. Study of the children's responses following their return to school after their Ancient Egypt experience certainly shows just how dramatic an impact such an event can have on young children.

The didactic introductory section was almost universally listened to with full attention. A remark made later on by one of the children:

I didn't know they had rivers in Egypt, I thought it was all sand with just a few lakes.

revealed one serious misconception that had been corrected as a result of the introduction.

The children afterwards wrote, some of them at considerable length, about the things they had enjoyed best, in some cases decorating the border of their written work to show some of the things they had learned. Some children described both on paper and orally the things they had made in their own time after they had returned home such as Egyptian jewellery (which had clearly been a big hit), and a model of a mummy in a sarcophagus.

The experiential learning as well as being an enjoyable experience, yielded dividends in the form of a clear understanding of the processes by which papyrus is made:

> You can find the reeds in Egypt by the River nile and in some swamps by the river nile. We had to fold the reeds down layer after layer and the glue in the reeds stuck the reeds together. Then we banged it down with a hammer. Then we had to rub a pebble on the reeds to make it shine.

It was clear from the accounts that the children subsequently wrote that they had clearly understood the processes in making papyrus along with other experiences, including the designing and making of jewellery and the creation of a life-size fresco. The opportunities provided had offered much more than mere observation of pictures or even the artefacts themselves could have provided.

To summarise the educational opportunities that staged events offer, we will consider first the learning at the children's level and secondly, what the student teachers gained from this experience, coming as it did at an early point in their training.

For the children, there are opportunities to build on existing knowledge and perceptions of other peoples and other times. They have a chance to engage in empathetic role play (in some cases wearing costumes) bearing appropriate names and in some cases handling relevant artefacts. Sometimes they are presented with quite difficult concepts and value issues which would make little impact on them if they were presented in more traditional ways. They experience travelling through time and in some cases have opportunities for decision making. The children all get some experience of working as young historians with primary sources. Children who have been identified by their school as having special educational needs respond particularly well to this approach. Student teachers, on the other hand, have the opportunity to think in some detail about the application of their chosen subject specialism at primary school level.

## Reflections on the use of role play and experiential learning

*Visiting museums*

Sometimes individual teachers have used a form of event as a way of bringing museums to life for their pupils. In the account of an event based on Ancient Egypt, it was shown how children gained much more from experiencing the process of making simulated papyrus than being merely allowed to observe examples of the finished article.

A junior school teacher, Sarah Foxton, was encouraged to attempt what she termed an interactive approach to museum visits after hearing what her children had to say about traditional museum visits:

> Museums are not very good because they are boring. They always got old things there. Nothing else. It smells of dead people. You're never allowed to touch nothing. I don't know why the Q's [sic] are so long because museums are boring. Museums are too quiet. They should have music in the background to make them better.

To provide a museum visit with a more interactive approach, this teacher involved her children in a role play before visiting the museum itself. She used this technique successfully with two different classes in preparation for visits to the Roman Baths at Bath and the Tudor period Red Lodge in Bristol.

Sarah found that the involvement of children in role play enabled them to prepare well for their visit, helping them to anticipate unfamiliar concepts and sensitising them to the great antiquity of the site that they were about to visit (including the fact that the Latin language was used in Roman times). She noticed that when the children visited the actual Roman Baths they used the Roman terms for each room. One Year 3 girl remarked:

> It's getting hotter. I think we must be getting to the Caldarium.

A boy in the same class commenting on a mosaic floor at the Baths said:

> Miss... it's amazing to think that one day real, real Romans walked along that piece of pavement.

*Staged events as a focus for role play and hands on activities*

The two authors who were involved in the Kwaku Ananse project (*see* above) built on their empathetic treatment of the story material to organise a series of joint cross-curricular activities over a 14 week period. Their objectives were as follows:

- First, to enable two schools with multi-racial intakes to co-operate on a joint venture.
- Second, to build on work already done by a Ghanaian tutor from the locally based Ekome Arts Group.
- Third, to create a context within which children were able to explore actively some aspects of Ghanaian life and culture, including story-telling, children's toys and games, agriculture and relations with first world countries.
- Fourth, to encourage children through participation in play making to think about issues arising from a project relating to building a dam on the River Volta.
- Fifth, to provide opportunities for children to be involved in music making, costume making, traditional dancing and the re-telling of stories.
- Sixth, to enable children to be placed in a new learning context alongside adults who are not normally members of their schools' teaching staff.

The collaborative programme was really a series of events spread over the 14 weeks, and included drama sessions, music making and dyeing workshops, in which a number of aspects of Ghanaian culture were explored through 'hands on' experience. Children had opportunities, for example, to make their own costumes using batik and tie-dyed patterns, to use block printing and paste resist techniques in the traditional styles of West Africa (*see* front cover and Figures 8.3 and 8.4).

*Learning about the Aztecs*

The final section of this chapter will bring together some of the issues raised earlier using the Aztecs as a focus. The requirement laid upon schools to teach primary-school children about the Aztecs and the Conquistadors, which originally appeared in Core Study Unit 6, has provided an exciting challenge to enormous numbers of teachers, who rarely ventured further into this topic than the voyages of Columbus, Drake, Raleigh and possibly John Cabot. The structure of this unit gave positive encouragement to teachers to develop the topic of the sixteenth-century encounters between European explorers and their American contemporaries in ways which related well to the three History Attainment Targets as originally conceived in the Statutory Orders. Here was a splendid opportunity to look at two peoples, with totally different cultures, neither of whom knew that the other existed. Here was a society whose capital city was vastly greater than the contemporary London of Henry VIII. This was, furthermore, a city which recycled human waste

156

**Figure 8.3** Kwaku Anansi: a drama production

**Figure 8.4** T-shirt designs: a child's clothes-line

and whose remarkable network of canals and lofty religious buildings were seen for the first time through the eyes of mariners who were familiar with the canals of Venice and with the cathedrals of Europe. There is sufficient primary source material available to provide opportunities not only for looking at this topic from different perspectives but also for studying in a vivid way the limitations as well as the value of historical evidence. The unit is also rich in possibilities for cross-curricular development including links with geography and RE.

It is noteworthy that the word 'discovery' which once characterised this episode in history was not used by the History Working Group and that its use has subsequently been avoided in the Statutory Orders. Among the general public and sadly among some teachers and students the notion that European explorers 'discovered' the Americas still prevails. There has been some recent debate about whether or not a group of Bristolian fishermen in search of cod in fact reached the Americas a few years before Christopher Columbus. Whichever side one comes down on in this debate, we now regard these hardy adventurers as early European visitors to America's shores rather than discoverers. In any case, were not the Vikings even earlier visitors from Europe around the year AD 1000?

A further problem with the teaching of this period is the continuing tendency to look at the Aztecs from a wholly Eurocentric viewpoint. In one school a teacher was recently heard preparing her children for a study of the religious beliefs and practices of the Aztecs by using such value-laden language as:

**It wasn't very nice at all. They used to do something disgusting ... they never washed their hair, they never washed the steps that were covered in blood.**

Such a view no doubt reflects the continuing perspective of European Christendom. It is understandable that, at first, we may feel revolted by the religious practices of the Aztecs; however, modern scholars in the field such as Clendinnen (1991), have sought to make the extraordinary and bloody rituals of the Aztec priests comprehensible within the particularly close-knit culture of ancient Mexico. The reactions of the Spanish conquistadors, as exemplified in the writings of Cortez and Dias need to be seen in their particular historical context, a context in which the Spanish could hardly be seen as blameless participants!

Another teacher, Marion Loveridge, planned her work on the Exploration and Encounters unit to culminate in a staged event. Marion decided to use role play as a means of developing empathy in her 9-year-old pupils. As a preliminary she carried out a series of exercises using primary source materials. Building on work by Harnett (1991) she encouraged the children carefully to scrutinise the pictures and to ask themselves what was happening in each of them. The pictures consisted of drawings which were all close in date to the actual conquest of Mexico. The children made the following perceptive comments:

**This painting is very biased towards the Spaniards because the**

158

artist has made them all look very magnificent in their armour on horseback.

It all depends on the artist's point of view. Maybe if this picture had been painted by someone else, then it would have looked completely different, especially if that person had liked the Aztecs better.

The children then went on to read the eyewitness evidence of Cortez and Dias. Marion recorded that these two accounts caused quite a stir:

Wow, these were written by people who were actually there!

I expect he was with the Spaniards when they went to Mexico to try and convert the Aztecs to Christianity. We'll have to make sure that we include a monk or a priest in our role play.

As noted earlier, it is impossible for us, living as we do in the later twentieth century, to really become part of the past. However, meticulous study of surviving sources can get us closer to events and everyday practices in the past.

*Using information technology*

Before concluding this chapter, it is important to make brief reference to the role which information technology can fulfil as a 'way in' to some of the approaches which have been discussed above.

During 1991–92, three Avon primary school teachers developed the Exploration and Encounters topic in their own schools as part of a collaborative venture linked to the Faculty of Education at the University of the West of England and funded by the National Council for Educational Technology. A central intention of this externally funded project was to generate ways of using information technology in conjunction with this particular study unit.

The Faculty's role had been to supply copies of several software programmes and to consider alongside their primary teacher colleagues ways in which the microcomputer might be used to assist learning in the classroom whilst this particular topic was being studied. Particularly fruitful were applications of *Touch Explorer Plus*, a facility more commonly used at Key stage 1, and the newsroom simulation *Extra*.

The former programme enables teachers to design their own overlay sheets for a concept keyboard attached to a microcomputer. A picture drawn on the overlay can be investigated by children by putting pressure with their fingers on particular parts of the illustration. As each feature of the picture is touched, details appear on the monitor screen. It is also possible for children to go beyond the surface features and to investigate the image at different 'levels'. Thus the research team had designed one overlay to represent a plan of the great temple of Tenochtitlan and surrounding parts of the Aztec capital and another to represent a Spanish ship. Each of these overlays provided the possibility of setting up a role play. For example, the ship could be explored not only in terms of the different parts of the ship such as the captain's quarters and the stores, but in terms of the different members of the crew and their respective roles on board ship. The newsroom simulation was programmed to issue at irregular intervals news items relating to the arrival of Spanish ships off the Eastern coast of Mexico. Each news item was presented from the point of view of the Aztecs who had never seen ships before, or people on horseback and who were totally unprepared for a technology which used the wheel, smelted iron and gunpowder.

Another application of IT which was used during a staged event in which all three schools participated, was the 'roamer' which was used by groups of children as a means of simulating the journey across the Atlantic.

One teacher, Joyce Richards, used *Extra* to provide a time machine. She recorded a series of historical events and their associated dates onto the program and encouraged her pupils to travel back in time to Mexico in 1521. Her class spent the whole day working on this project. As each event was announced on the screen, the class moved back a little further in time and became involved in a series of collaborative discussions and investigations using a variety of resources.

Another teacher, Bob Callicott, used a piece of software, *Teletype,* to present two perspectives on events which would run alongside each other. The pupils were divided into two halves: one group were Aztecs awaiting news of the invaders' progress, whilst the other group represented Spanish reporters eager to transmit news from the 'front', to their home country. Both groups had to produce a newspaper for distribution in their respective countries. The simulation ran for one and a half hours, during which time the children were fully absorbed working non-stop using books, pictures, posters, postcards and videotapes. This was an opportunity for looking at first-hand evidence such as contemporary writings, pictures and at the results of recent archaeological excavations. The only problem that arose was that the Aztec group did not really want to find out about the Spaniards. They were more interested in researching Aztec life, mainly because it was so different.

## Conclusion

In this chapter, we have attempted to explore a variety of ways in which the teaching of primary school humanities can be tackled by developing an empathetic approach and through the use of various forms of active learning. The more elaborate form of staged event has also been described in some detail, with a view to demonstrating how effective an approach this can be for both children and adults as learners. The opportunities for schools to work in collaboration on a staged event has also been described and the possibilities for information technology to play a part in promoting these opportunities has been included.

Many of the ideas and activities devised for use in the context of staged events can, however, be used in the form suggested or with adaptations by teachers in their own schools and classrooms (*see* Figure 8.5 for further examples).

---

## Historical events undertaken at UWE involving children

**Ancient Greece**
- Athenian democracy
- a school
- the palaestra
- rowing on a trireme
- puppetry and a Greek myth
- visit to the Delphic Oracle

**Invaders and Settlers**

**Roman**
- a visit to Aquae Sulis (Roman Bath)
- the bathing establishment
- offerings at the Sacred Spring
- Roman games (indoor)
- making mosiacs
- outdoor exercises

**Saxon**
- the burial of King Redwald
- writing
- story-telling
- cooking
- producing artefacts
- music making

**Tudor England**
- the Spanish Armada
- education in Tudor times

**Aztecs**
- building the great temple tower
- IT activities
- using roamer technology to cross the Atlantic
- festival of Etzalqualitzli
- prayers to Tlaloc, the rain god

**Victorian Britain**
- visit of Queen Victoria to Bristol using local environment

**Ancient Egypt**
- the reign of the female Pharoah

---

**Figure 8.5** Historical events undertaken at UWE involving children

# CHAPTER NINE

# Humanities in the Primary Classroom – The Role of the Teacher

This chapter will review what we know about the ways in which children learn and relate this knowledge about how children learn to humanities teaching.

We begin by looking at the familiar argument on whether to start from children's immediate environments or from elsewhere when teaching humanities. The teacher's role in organising and assessing learning is then discussed. In the next part of the chapter the centrality of talk in the learning process is emphasised. Finally we consider general approaches to curriculum planning and classroom organisation.

## The child as a starting-point

All children possess a wealth of knowledge on which the humanities teacher can build. The teacher has a key role in assessing children's existing understanding and in recognising the different contributions which children bring to the learning process. The extract below illustrates the responses of 6–7-year-old children during a brainstorming session introduced by their teacher to ascertain their current knowledge and understanding of the Ancient Egyptians.

James:     They put kings in white bandages.
Asghar:    Mummies.
James:     They had pyramids with secret doors to hide treasure.
Asghar:    Cleopatra's treasure was wheat.
Suleiman:  ...treasure was carried on camels.
Mukhtyar:  ...traps to stop thieves getting to the treasure.

162

| | |
|---|---|
| *Wendy:* | ...camels went to far-away cities. |
| *James:* | ...they put people in rivers when they died. |
| *Suleiman:* | ...they built a temple for the king when he dies. |
| *James:* | ...some kings were buried in pyramids. |
| *Mukhtyar:* | ....they were hidden so no one could see their buried treasure. |
| *Kendra:* | ...jewels in far away mines. |
| *Pat:* | ....diamonds |
| *Mukhtyar:* | ....gold |
| *Suleiman:* | ....buried kings in temples. |
| *Asghar:* | ...did hand dances [demonstrates typical hand movements for the dance of the seven veils] |
| *Kendra:* | ...they had a triangle thing with steps [pyramid] |
| *Asghar:* | ...statue of a half cat and half woman. Legends of spirits. |
| *James:* | Tutankhamen's death mask. |

This brainstorm shows a mixture of correct information and some stereotyped information (which might also be shared by adults). For example, camels were unknown in Ancient Egypt. The child who imitated the hand movements of an Egyptian dance copied a common misrepresentation drawn from popular media.

Asked how they knew so much about the Ancient Egyptians, these children explained their sources as: 'my sister'; 'the bible'; 'my mind'; 'books'; 'television'; 'museum' and 'children's adventures on TV'.

Children do not live in a vacuum. They are surrounded by information supplied by different media which takes them beyond their immediate environment. Television conveys images of far-away places, of people grappling with events and difficulties outside the personal experience of most children. The danger is that popular culture may also provide representations which are misleading and inaccurate.

Children's learning at school needs to take into account their experiences of the wider world. We have moved away from the Victorian classroom where children could be seen as 'empty vessels', to be filled up from the teachers' vast stores of knowledge. The complexity of the learning process is more fully recognised now. Although discounted in theory, this 'empty vessel' view of teaching and learning tends to persist. Unless recognition is given to children's experiences outside school, and time is created for children to express their existing understanding and knowledge, children could feel themselves undervalued and learn that it is only what they are taught in school which counts as worthwhile.

Teachers play a crucial role in valuing children's existing knowledge. They can also provide activities where children can synthesise their different learning experiences and begin to make sense of them by placing them within a broader understanding.

The example of the Ancient Egyptians illustrates that children can explore and can be excited by unfamiliar material which is far removed from their own experience. Often teachers try to mediate the unfamiliar and strange by creating links with what they perceive as children's existing understanding. However, as the following extract indicates, there are dangers in making such assumptions:

> A student planned to tell a group of 6-year-old children about the Great Fire of London. Before the story began she set the scene carefully. Children were asked if they had heard of London, where it was, what they could see there, if they had ever visited the city and gradually a picture of London was built up. The children listened with interest to the ensuing story about the Great Fire. As the fire took hold, the student held up a picture of what was happening in Pudding Lane. A child who had been listening attentively called out, 'Where's my Auntie Bett?'

Of course Auntie Bett was nowhere to be seen. She lived in the London of the 1990s, not 1666! The student had sought to introduce the story against a background of a familiar context, i.e. contemporary London. However, this introduction created further misunderstanding for the child as to when the Great Fire actually occurred and who was there at the time.

This example highlights how our perceptions of how children learn and our assumptions of children's current understanding can create difficulties in planning for their learning in the classroom. The student had begun with what she perceived as the children's familiar experiences, but these had only served to mislead and confuse as the comment from the child enquiring about Auntie Bett reveals.

Such confusions are related to the notion of what Richard Eke (1986) has called 'Lego thinking'. He argues that most children in a primary-school classroom know that just because a house made of Lego can be taken to bits it does not necessarily mean that it would be necessary or always desirable to put it back together in the same way. However he suggests that:

> most curriculum planners including teachers are willing to break down curriculum Lego in this way on the grounds that this makes it easier for the children to reconstruct this knowledge into a more or less suitable substitute for the original edifice. (Eke, 1986:8)

Children working in the humanities are often are faced with concepts and ideas of which they can have little or no first-hand experience, for example castles, volcanoes or different belief systems. We turn now to examine how children try to make sense of new ideas and concepts and to incorporate them within their current understandings.

*Familiar or the Unknown?*

Seated on the carpet, 3- and 4-year-olds review what they have been learning about the Plains Indians. In this extract we focus on the children. More of the teacher's contribution is added in and commented on later.

*Teacher:* They had teepees. [Teacher pauses]
*Katie:* They had poles to start with and then skin from the buffaloes.
*James:* When they want to catch people they use swords. They needed guns to catch people as well.
*Richard:* They had hammerhawks.
*James:* My grandad uses a chain saw to cut down trees.
*Teacher:* I wonder if the Indians had chain saws.
*All:* No – axes.
*Philip:* When they want to pull down a tree they made string into rope and put it down and if they were too close they would get squashed.

The discussion continued:
*James:* The North Americans fighted against the Indians and soldiers tried to get their land.
*Philip:* No the white people and they did get the Indians land and in the end all the Indians were killed and they put their bows on the ground.
*Teacher:* Where do they live?
*Jane:* In North America where Father Christmas lives.
*Philip:* You would travel over sea and land and desert as well.

The discussion continued on tepees and the children commented that they did not live in tepees all the time.
*Maria:* They packed their tepees like a tent.
*Philip:* They put them in knapsacks and they roll them up.
*Richard:* My grandpa goes camping.
*Philip:* They carried the poles in their hands and the rest in their knapsacks.
*Katie:* My tent is a square tent.
*Andrew:* My tent is a triangle with wooden poles.
*Sean:* There was a hole at the top for smoke to come out.
*Jane:* They had a fire in the tepee.
*Katie:* It was for keeping them warm.
*Jane:* ...and cooking.

*Teacher:* ...and we have cookers and a fire.
*Philip:*　I've got a hundred radiators in my house.

In this extract the children can be seen making connections between the old and the new, linking fresh information with familiar situations. The transcript reveals the highly personal and idiosyncratic way in which individuals make sense of their world. For example Philip talked of the radiators in his house, James mentioned his grandfather's chain saw and Katie talked about her tent.

Not only were the children being asked to comment on a different way of life, they were also sharing ideas about the passage of time, 'in the olden days', distance, 'a land far away' and to the motives behind human actions – 'the soldiers tried to get their land'. The classroom environment supported the children's learning (Figure 9.1). In their nursery class these children were being introduced to some of the key issues in humanities education.

**Figure 9.1** Nursery children learning about Plains Indians

Theories of child development stemming from the work of Piaget have tended to underestimate young children's abilities to deal with such issues. In the past, teachers adhering to the series of structured sequential stages described by Piaget would have been more likely to impose limits on children's learning experiences, believing that young children would not have the capacity to explore ideas and situations of which they had not had some direct and concrete experience. However, the work of more recent psychologists – Margaret Donaldson (1978) for example – has demonstrated the importance of context in children's thinking. Such work has revealed that, given the appropriate context, children's capacities for abstract thinking and logical reasoning are more developed than was generally thought previously. It is to such writers that we will now turn to consider the planning and organisation of learning in the classroom.

Grieve and Hughes (1990) have suggested a number of implications for education, deriving from Donaldson's work. They emphasise:

(a) The importance of considering the whole child, and the learning process, from the child's point of view. The importance of both social and cultural contexts must be addressed.

(b) The need to help children move from embedded thought, relating to particular contexts, to the more abstract representations of knowledge that they encounter in school, and the disembedded thought of the adult world.

These insights have implications for classroom practice and are considerations which should guide a teacher's planning and organisation. They are discussed more fully below.

*Developing children's pathways to understanding*

In earlier chapters we have emphasised the highly personal nature of the children's responses and sought to examine learning as Grieve and Hughes (1990) advocate from the child's point of view. In the example at the beginning of the chapter only a few 6–7 year olds were able to supply any information for the brainstorm on the Ancient Egyptians, however the whole class was enthusiastic to know more. In pairs they compiled a whole range of questions. They included enquiries about:

- temples and pyramids and their construction;
- mummies and the rituals of the dead;
- details about domestic life in Egyptian times;
- life beside the river Nile.

The initial brainstorm to which only a few children had contributed acted as a stimulus for the whole class. Questions were generated which revealed that the children were capable of organising their own agenda for learning, stemming from their own interests.

Personal responses must be valued. As they grow older many children subsume their own ideas and offer only what they think the teacher wants them to say, engaging in an 'answer hunt' (whether they see them as relevant or not) since 'right answers' pay off. John Holt (1965:96) suggests real dangers in schools becoming 'a kind of temple of worship for "right answers", and the way to get ahead is to lay plenty of them on the altar.'

The above examples illustrate points arising in looking at learning from children's viewpoints. Teachers have a key role in investigating children's perspectives and in assessing their current understandings and opinions about their work. We turn now to examine some of the ways in which teachers might study children's perceptions.

## Assessing children's pathways

Assessment, its place at the heart of the learning process, and its essential role in planning and in identifying difficulties has been implicit in all the studies which we have described in this book. Understanding the place of assessment in our education system makes demands on teacher thinking, both morally and philosophically. In Drummond's words the practice of effective assessment:

> requires a thorough understanding and acceptance of the concepts of rights, responsibility and power, lying at the heart of our work as teachers.
> (1993:11)

It is not within the remit of this book to provide a comprehensive guide on assessment in the humanities. What we wish to do is simply to:

(a) consider the purpose of assessment;
(b) look at values and principles associated with assessment in the humanities;
(c) consider how we gather and record evidence for assessment in the humanities.

### The purpose of assessment

In recent years a great deal of concern on the part of central government has been directed towards the raising of educational standards. One tool that is purported to serve this purpose is a particular kind of assessment which seeks to establish a set of objective targets against which children can be measured. Parents can then be informed of their children's achievements in these tests.

This is not the prime purpose of assessment, in our view. The implicit role of assessment in all the case studies described in this book is one where:

> we can use our assessments to shape and enrich our curriculum, our interactions, our provision as a whole; we can use our assessments as a way of identifying what children will learn next, so that we can support and extend that learning. Assessment is part of our daily lives in striving for quality.
> (Drummond 1993:13)

*Principles of assessment in the humanities*

Blyth (1990) writes about approaches to assessment in primary humanities, and has attempted to explore the relationship between knowledge and understanding. He makes a clear distinction between 'recall' and 'transfer', that is between rote learning and its application to other situations.

He also considers that assessment in the humanities has four major aspects which should be considered as separate processes: skills, concepts, values and attitudes, and task procedures. These processes are distinct but interlink with each other.

The aspects which Blyth emphasises reflect both the cognitive and affective domains. If we are encouraging children to consider what is special about being human then they will be strongly involved in raising questions of values and attitudes, expressing concerns and developing a sense of responsibility towards others. In Chapter 3 we included children's views on the fairness of prices paid as a result of trading between western and non-western countries. Chapter 5 records children's responses to the situation and needs of the homeless.

To undertake assessment in the humanities we need to have a view on what constitutes progress and achievement – progress in developing skills, handling concepts and knowledge and also in developing positive and responsible attitudes. To develop their own understanding and to make informed decisions on subsequent action, teachers must plan opportunities for collecting evidence of children's learning.

*Gathering evidence for assessment*

Campbell and Little (1989) emphasise that effective assessment of the humanities is focused on the acquired capacities and understandings of children's learning rather than their factual knowledge.

They emphasise that this can only be achieved by monitoring classroom activities and not by formal testing.

It is also important to use a variety of ways of collecting evidence so that particular children are not constantly disadvantaged by the use of the same technique. All the case studies in this book supply evidence of children's learning, and indicate forms in which it might be collected: drawing and writing, drama, role play, concept mapping, the use of floorbooks and brainstorming.

Examples of talking, listening and of structuring activities to encourage debate have also been included. Keeping samples of work in a central portfolio is fundamental to the process of assessment. At school level policies need to be agreed upon so that this can be done effectively and to inform curriculum planning and classroom organisation. Children can be assessed not only in terms of their knowledge and conceptual understanding but also in terms of their enthusiasm and the significance they attach to their learning. Pupil self-assessment is a useful vehicle here. Following a successful lesson on making water clocks a class of 8–9-year-old children were asked to carry out an evaluation of the activity. This evaluation comprised answering a series of questions about the process that had taken place:

(a) Which parts of the work did you like best?
(b) Which were most difficult to understand?
(c) What particular new ideas and information did you learn?
(d) Did you think you were able to express your thoughts and feelings clearly?

This list is not suggested as a definitive one. Many writers have written more fully about children evaluating activities and self-assessment. However, one child's response is revealing:

I learnt to do something without feeling stupid.

This comment is a stark reminder of how teachers have the power to influence children's feelings of self-esteem and also how this self-assessment can support children with differing levels of achievement.

*Assessment as a support for the learner*
The illustration above indicates that assessment is not only a tool for teachers. Self-evaluation and assessment can also be powerful aids for the learners themselves. At the University of West England students are encouraged to reflect on their own practice and learning. The benefits of this process are illustrated in the previous chapter, where students were asked to identify what they felt they had learnt following an Ancient Egyptian day. Their evaluations included comments on how they felt their knowledge about the Ancient Egyptians had increased and how they had developed their skills in handling children. Interestingly too, many students evaluated the event in terms of increasing their self-confidence and developing more positive relationships with their fellow students. Such observations remind us once again of the very personal nature of the learning process.

## Extending children's understandings: the importance of talk

Examples from case studies have enabled us to identify elements of learning in the humanities: knowledge, concepts, skills and values. Cross-curricular links and the relationship of different subject areas within the curriculum have been identified and a place for humanities within the National Curriculum subjects recognised. One of the many challenges facing us as teachers is to find ways which enable children to encounter these different elements meaningfully and to support children's progress into the more abstract representations of the adult world. The role of talk is fundamental in so many of these approaches.

## The knowledgeable other

In this chapter, the case studies of the Ancient Egyptians and Plains Indians reveal some of the children's understandings. Identifying children's interests and existing perceptions is important if we are to help children to move across their current zone of proximal development towards a deeper understanding. As more knowledgeable others, our broader perspective on the subject enables us to move children further forward.

This point can be made clearer by referring back to the 6 and 7 year olds learning about the Ancient Egyptians. The children raised many questions about the Ancient Egyptians yet no child indicated a desire to know when they lived. The teacher felt the time dimension was important and later was able to encourage her children to think about it too. Her broader knowledge of the subject enabled her to draw children's attention to the difficult concept of thousands of years, something which they might not have explored on their own. The teacher approached this difficulty by striding out the centuries in the playground until a long line of equally spaced infants visually depicted the passage of time from now back to the Ancient Egyptians. The children could count the centuries back to the Ancient Egyptians!

If we take into account their starting-points, and present experiences, children really can learn about complex ideas and far off things. This view of the curriculum is supported by Bruner (1960) who argued that:

> ...any subject can be taught effectively in some intellectually honest form to any child at any stage of development. (1960:33)

This is well illustrated by the nursery-aged children engaged on the cross-curricular topic of the Plains Indians. In this example young children were able to include different contexts quite spontaneously. They incorporated learning acquired in other contexts when they explored fresh information about the Plains Indians. In the tepee, where they played at keeping house, comments such as, 'have a slice of buffalo' were recorded. On construction activities children were keen to build tepees. They looked closely at face markings when they came to design and paint their own Indian masks. They recognised that their models were only representations too.

*Philip:* This is our totem pole – we painted it and put milk bottle tops on it. The Indians would have painted them though.

In the past, planning for progression in humanities and the assessment implicit in this planning has not been in the foreground of teachers' work. Alexander, Rose and Woodhead commented in 1992:

> that there is no doubt that much topic work has been and still is very undemanding, particularly in History and Geography. Too many topics amount to little more than aimless and superficial copying from books and offer pupils negligible opportunities for progression from one year to the next. (Alexander *et al.*, 1992:22).

However, when work is well planned and teachers are aware of what they are trying to promote in terms of the children's learning (knowledge, concepts, skills and values), humanities teaching can be very effective. At Key Stage 1 this planning may take a cross-curricular format as illustrated in the Plains Indians above. At Key Stage 2, it may have a stronger subject focus. HMI have indicated that particularly at Key Stage 2, where schools have incorporated a 2-, 3- or 4-year cycle into their planning, with a different emphasis (on geography, history or science):

> there was some evidence to show that this brought about more systematic teaching of the "lead" subject and a general improvement in the quality of topic work. (HMI, 1994:5)

Several examples in this book have been included to illustrate the links which can be made between humanities and the core subjects. In Chapter 3, as the children worked on their maps, they were also being introduced to several mathematical ideas linked with shape and space. Later in the same chapter, scientific ideas linked with materials and changes of state could have been developed as the children investigated volcanoes. Opportunities taken to develop written and spoken language have been described in many examples.

We turn now to consider the organisation of learning in the humanities at classroom level. The examples of children working in the humanities have drawn on different forms of classroom organisation. Whole class sessions have been included, together with instances where children have worked collaboratively in groups, independently and also with the teacher. We begin by returning to some of the points from Chapter 1 where we considered how children might best learn in the humanities.

*Children learning together*

Active learning has been a recurrent feature in many of the case studies in this book. With respect to the humanities, active learning can be considered in two ways:

(a) In the familiar sense of children being involved in practical and investigational activities, often interacting and collaborating with others, i.e. within the classroom set-up.

(b) In the sense of taking action. Children exercising a sense of responsibility by engaging in action to try to seek solutions and improve situations. An example can be seen in Chapter 6 where children are described demonstrating to support a new bypass to reduce traffic and air pollution near their homes. A further example is in Chapter 5, where children write letters to seek help and support for the homeless, i.e. reaching out into the real world of other human beings.

We have already emphasised the importance of the social and cultural context in the learning process. In the initial brainstorm on the Ancient Egyptians described at the beginning of this chapter, a few children provided the stimulus which engaged the whole class. The class responded eagerly to the invitation to work in pairs and think of more questions. As they worked together they supported each other in trying to find out more. In this instance, the children were seen as active social beings, interacting with each other and with their environment. This is a powerful way of working and draws heavily on Vygotsky's learning paradigm.

> What a child can do today in co-operation, tomorrow he will be able to do on his own. (Vygotsky, 1962)

We have sought to demonstrate the importance of the social nature of learning; case study material has included comments from children and students as they work together.

Arranging children in different groups is a common feature in primary classrooms. However, it would appear that grouping children is seen by teachers to be more of an organisational device than a tool for learning. Galton *et al.* (1980) found that while most children sat in groups, most of their time was spent on individual tasks, and they spent approximately two-thirds of their time interacting with no one. Tizard *et al.* (1988) found that group work of the kind encouraged in this book, involving children working co-operatively on a task or activity, occurred rarely in the sample of infant classrooms studied.

It is often not enough to place children (or have them place themselves) in groups. In most cases strategies have to be developed in order to teach children how to work co-operatively and to support each other.

Many teachers are aware of the complex challenge which collaborative working presents. In Avon (1993a) there has been a radical move to introduce children to the social and process skills which enable them to participate fully in collaborative work. This was through a structured framework which reflected the 'High Scope' Plan-Do-Review cycle (Figure 9.2).

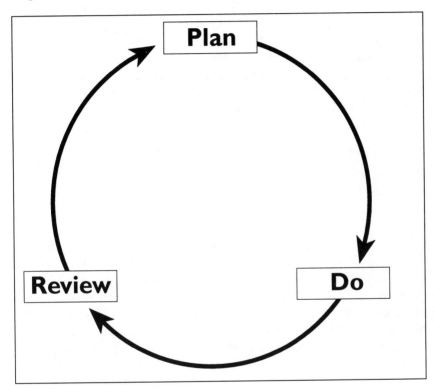

**Figure 9.2** The High Scope cycle

These strategies could be used to enhance language and reading skills but could equally well be used as a vehicle for developing collaborative learning in the humanities.

Biott and Easden (1994:202) suggest that one of the major difficulties in collaborative work is that the place of conflict is misunderstood. Conflict can make a positive contribution: it is more appropriate to regard collaborative working as a 'deconstructive learning process' where children, by talking together can make 'thinking explicit' and build up a fund of common knowledge or understanding in addition to challenging their existing ideas.

Such strategies as described in the Avon project enable teachers to confront the problematic nature of collaborative activity which can lead to a re-definition of the teacher's traditional instructor role. In classrooms where collaborative group work is actively encouraged, the teacher becomes more of a facilitator and organiser of learning experiences which contrasts with a rather more conventional interpretation of the teacher having a role as the fount of all knowledge in the classroom.

Recent research by Bennett and Dunne (1992) has emphasised the value of structuring group work in the classroom. Improvements were seen to occur in classrooms when teachers systematically planned for co-operative group work. Children were seen to be more involved in their work and its quality was enhanced. The range and nature of children's talk was also extended. For teachers, Bennett and Dunne also noted the benefits which accrued from the creation of time, as teachers became less involved with requests from individual children.

*Teacher talk*

Providing opportunities for children to engage in the purposeful talk so vital to the learning process is a major consideration for planning work in the humanities.

However, this does not occur in all classrooms as research evidence reveals. Studies in the USA have suggested that two-thirds of the talk spent in teaching sessions, emanates from the teacher (Flanders, 1970). More recent studies in the UK have also supported these findings (Bennett *et al.*, 1984; Galton *et al.*, 1980). While teachers generate most of the talk in the classroom, it follows that children are doing most of the listening. The PACE project (Pollard *et al.*, 1994) findings reveal infant children interacting with their teacher for about 40% of the working day, about 35% of which is as part of the whole class when children are listening. These findings provide an interesting contrast with those of the ORACLE study mentioned earlier (Galton *et al.*, 1980) found junior children spending 12% of their time interacting with the teacher and most of this time was spent in listening.

Interaction by the teacher with individual children has been found to be very limited. Galton *et al.* (1980) concluded that junior teachers interacted on an individual basis with a child for just over 2% of the time. Tizard *et al.* (1988) reached similar conclusions from their observations of infant classrooms. The quality of this limited teacher–pupil interaction has also been investigated. The findings of Tizard *et al.* (1988) revealed that 80% of teacher talk involved communicating facts and ideas, and very little talk centred on social or personal contact or praise. Similar findings have emerged from the Primary Needs Project in Leeds

(PRINDEP, 1990); well over a third of all teacher interactions were concerned with the content of the tasks which had been set; marking, checking and monitoring progress accounting for a further third of the teacher interactions.

Literature abounds with examples of children's misunderstandings of adult language; one famous example is that of Laurie Lee in *Cider with Rosie* attending school for the first time. He is asked to 'sit there for the present' and is very disappointed when the present has not arrived by the end of the day!

The following extract illustrates a similar point.

> The reception teacher had planned an interesting movement lesson for her group of children. Moving around the apparatus in the hall, the children were to practise different movements and to concentrate on their body shapes. The lesson had gone well; children had listened carefully to instructions and had enjoyed the activities. As Richard left the hall he was asked what he did in movement lessons, his response was, 'I learnt to be quiet.'

The child in this extract had focused his attention on only part of the lesson; the teacher **had** demanded that the children work quietly, but she had also taken great care to explain the different movements which she wanted the children to try. Richard's learning agenda and consequent behaviour during the lesson only partially matched the full expectations of the teacher.

The above example is not an isolated case; children are exposed to teacher language of which, at times they may only have a partial understanding. Research evidence supports this view (Barnes, 1976). Creating communication procedures whereby teacher and children can share understandings and attach similar meanings to the learning process are important. At times teachers may employ specialised terms and vocabulary before they have acquired sufficient meaning within children's conceptual understandings. Such concepts as before, after, profit, citizenship and location should be developed from concrete experience. Throughout the book we have given examples of children dealing with specialised and technical terms but only when such vocabulary has been introduced to them in a way in which they can understand. For example, at first, child K mentioned that the Ancient Egyptians had 'a triangle thing with steps', but by the end of the lesson she was confident in her use of the term pyramid.

Evidence suggests that most talk in the classroom emanates from the teacher and there appears to be little opportunity for children's exploratory talk. Question and answer sessions may predominate. Moreover, the PRINDEP (1990) study provides evidence to suggest that these questions are often at a low level, providing little encouragement for children to work systematically through an idea or build on their existing understanding.

The National Oracy Project (Norman, 1990) has sought to create fundamental shifts in attitude both for adults and children. Particular enabling roles for the teacher have been identified which include scaffolding children's understanding through dialogue and providing a role model for children, actively listening to what children say and making decisions about when to participate in group activities, acting as an audience and asking questions.

*Supporting children's talk*

Questions from the teacher can encourage information recall and can also probe and encourage children to extend their understandings. The High Scope Foundation (1979) suggest a range of techniques and strategies for supporting children's talk:

(a) Self-talk where the teacher describes and labels what she does.
(b) Parallel talk when the teacher describes what the child is doing.
(c) Repeating what the child has said.
(d) Restating. If the child has made an error repeating in the correct form without drawing attention to it – i.e. modelling the correct language.
(e) Expanding on the child's ideas.
(f) Encouraging ideas – asking children to describe what they have done, often by asking them to help you.
(g) Open-ended questions which can encourage a variety of solutions to a problem.

Some of these strategies can be quite clearly observed in the way the teacher structures her talk in the Plains Indians extract.

*Teacher:* They had tepees. [Teacher pauses]
*Katie:*   They had poles to start with and then skin from the buffaloes.
*Teacher:* Yes they used the skin from buffaloes.....
**(c: Teacher repeating what the child had said.)**
*James:*   When they want to catch people they use swords. They needed guns to catch people as well.
*Richard:* They had hammerhawks.
*Teacher:* Yes the Indians used tomahawks.
**(d: Teacher restating, repeating in the correct form without drawing attention to the error – modelling the correct language.)**

*James:* My granddad uses a chain saw to cut down trees.
*Teacher:* I wonder if the Indians had chain saws?
**(f: Teacher using open-ended questions which can encourage a variety of solutions to a problem.)**
*All:* No – axes.

Another useful framework for developing talk and language and for structuring children's ideas in the humanities, is provided by Antonouris and Wilson (1989) (Figure 9.3).

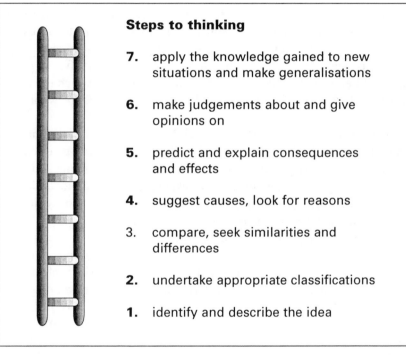

**Steps to thinking**

7. apply the knowledge gained to new situations and make generalisations

6. make judgements about and give opinions on

5. predict and explain consequences and effects

4. suggest causes, look for reasons

3. compare, seek similarities and differences

2. undertake appropriate classifications

1. identify and describe the idea

**Figure 9.3** Steps in thinking

The tasks listed here can be seen as a ladder for children to ascend as they develop their understanding about particular concepts and ideas. It might not be appropriate to climb all the rungs in all activities, but it is argued that using this ladder as a background for planning will help to guarantee that children are introduced to a variety of different thinking processes and that some continuity and coherence between different activities will be generated. As such, this ladder can provide some structure for teacher pupil, and pupil interaction in the humanities.

Using language is a dynamic activity. We learn and we can express ideas about what we have learnt through using language. Some of the discussions shown in this book have enabled the children to think out aloud, to wrestle with some of their ideas and to clarify their thoughts. Working in this way involves both speaking and listening skills. Individuals learn to present their own points of view and to express their ideas clearly. Listening skills are cultivated as the discussion develops and further social skills are acquired as individuals interact with each other. Discussion can involve children in quite abstract reasoning where they need to predict particular outcomes and to express themselves using tentative and speculative language where 'might be's' and possible alternatives are acknowledged.

We have seen how teachers can encourage learning in the humanities and support children in their spoken language. We turn now to discuss the development of children's reading and writing in the humanities.

History, geography, science and maths are all written in different genres and children need to become aware of the purposes for which the text is to be used, the form that it should take, and the audience for whom it is written.

Wray and Lewis (1994) describe children who are aware that they should not copy from existing texts and who are also able to give sensible reasons for this. Wray and Lewis maintain that factors limiting children's understanding are their limited knowledge of the topic and their difficulties with linguistic features (vocabulary, connectives, cohesion, register) of the reference books.

Members of the EXCEL project have been working in Junior schools helping teachers to develop a number of strategies for fostering children's information skills. In one such strategy which focuses on information retrieval the child is asked to brainstorm (either using words or diagrams) anything known about a particular topic. This is a recognition of children's existing knowledge and experience; it also provides an opportunity for assessment. Questions which might then be posed at various stages in the work might include: 'What do I know?'; 'What do I want to know?' and 'What have I learned?'. This provides a research structure and the child is much more able to return to the books and answer the questions. Self-esteem is enhanced and confidence built.

The following example illustrates how a group of Year 5 children used this technique as a midpoint review for their topic on Captain Scott. It enabled them to evaluate the extent of their learning and gave direction for their future research.

What we know:
1. Captain Scott was a man.
2. He wanted to get to the South Pole first.
3. Captain Scott wrote a diary.
4. The dogs fell down the cracks in the ice.

5. He had to build a hut and store food.
6. Captain Scott saw a black dot and as they got further they saw it was the Norwegian flag.
7. Four months later a search party came looking for them.
8. They had to make a special boat to get to the South Pole.
9. They had to wear special clothes so they did not get many frost bites.

What we want to find out:
1. I would like to find out what Scott wrote in his diary.
2. How old Captain Scott was when he went to the South Pole.
3. Where he was born.
4. When he was born.
5. What year it was when he decided to go to the South Pole.
6. What Captain Scott had to eat.

## Conclusion

The emphasis throughout this book has been on children working actively in the classroom. It has been exciting to describe how children have explored different topics and how they have made learning their own. The teacher's important role in this process must not be underestimated.

As humanities teachers it is important to recognise the nature of the subject we are teaching. Recognition will be given to particular skills and concepts we want to develop and the attitudes we would wish to foster in our children as they work. Knowledge, including a factual component, which can help children to extend their understandings, will also need be included.

In the introduction to this book we quote Rex Beddis who influenced a number of the authors. Beddis emphasised that amongst other things, humanities education was about beliefs, experience and behaviour. Thus a study of humanities will inevitably raise political questions and will not be value free. The study of humanities will involve discussion of conflicting ideas; a study of humanities will create tensions. To meet the challenge which humanities education presents it is necessary to ask a fundamental question: 'what kind of teacher am I?' Drummond (1993:112) maintains that asking this question:

> ...is a powerful exercise in making one's innermost values apparent: to ask oneself "why am I this kind of teacher?" is to take an even more important step to connecting one's internal value system to the external realities of children's learning in primary schools.

The Education Reform 1988 states that:

> the curriculum for a maintained school satisfies the requirements of this
> section if it is a balanced and broadly based curriculum which –
> (a) promotes the spiritual, moral, cultural, mental and physical development
>     of pupils at the school and of society and
> (b) prepares such pupils for the opportunities, responsibilities and
>     experiences of adult life.

The learning of humanities by its very nature must be a central part of this balanced and broadly based curriculum.

Case study material in the preceding chapters reveal teachers' awareness of this broad and balanced curriculum. These teachers recognise the importance of the knowledge base of their teaching as well as knowing how children best learn. Such teachers are expert in creating a democratic classroom environment. Humane values can be applied and diversity can be encouraged so that children can use their minds and valued for what they can contribute. We reject the picture of humanities education as it used to be taught. The impetus of back to basics, dates, capes and bays and good and evil, encouraging a narrow focus upon factual recall (easily assessed) must be resisted. A balanced and broadly based curriculum cannot be delivered in such a way.

Our evidence suggests that many teachers are imaginative and creative in their approach to teaching the humanities. They are always seeking pathways which enable them to mould the content of the National Curriculum and make it meaningful for the children they teach. We hope that this book has made a further contribution to their thinking and provided them with some additional signposts to develop their own pathways.

This Chapter has described some of challenges of teaching in the 1990s. Chapter 10 goes on to address those challenges of the future.

# CHAPTER TEN

# *Conclusion*

No one would remember the Good Samaritan if he'd only had good
intentions. He had money as well.

Margaret Thatcher, 6 January 1986

Throughout this book we have been concerned to identify the particular
contribution of the humanities to the learning of young children in the
primary school. In this concluding chapter we wish to look outside the school again and
to reconsider the wider social and political context within which primary
teachers are working and young children are learning. It is also an
opportunity to look ahead and consider possible developments in primary
humanities as we reach the Millennium.

The political settlement which was represented by the 1944 Education
Act (*see* Barber, 1994) was based on a broad consensus, no doubt fostered
by the experience of world war and a period of economic depression. It
was a consensus which enabled government, local authorities and
teachers to work together in partnership with commonly held aims for the
educational system. There is now little disagreement that by the 1970s
some aspects of the system were no longer adequately meeting the
requirements of a modern technological society.

Certainly the humanities subjects were relatively neglected in primary
schools throughout this time, although there were a few notable localised
exceptions. Surveys carried out by Her Majesty's Inspectors of Schools
(for example HMI, 1978:80), showed a great tendency for teachers to
concentrate almost exclusively on mathematics and English, with little
systematic attention being given to any other subjects. The emergence of
a 10- or 11-subject National Curriculum in 1988 can therefore be seen as
a very significant broadening of the primary curriculum. However, the
emphasis on subjects rather than for example on areas of experience (the

term used by HMI, 1985) did lead to the risk of the fragmentation of learning in the humanities.

The enormous new demands on primary teachers meant that they found great difficulty in managing the broader curriculum in an effective way. For example, the PACE study found teachers at Key Stage 1 frustrated and angry at the impossibility of covering the full range of curriculum content stipulated in the National Curriculum documents (Pollard *et al.*, 1994). Inspection reports and surveys which followed the implementation of the National Curriculum found considerable weaknesses in the teaching of history and geography (HMI, 1994).

The years since 1988 have seen considerable upheaval within the education system in England and Wales, not least in the rapid construction and then reconstruction of a national curriculum. We have considered different subjects and cross-curricular elements at various points in the book. Our purpose here is to step back and consider the curriculum as a whole and the place of humanities within it. The political rhetoric which accompanied the Dearing review of the National Curriculum promised a 'slimmed down' curriculum which would be 'manageable' and 'sensible'. The fact that this review coincided with a major government drive for a reassertion of traditional values – the infamous 'back to basics' campaign – has led some commentators, including many teachers, to fear not simply a slimmed down curriculum, but one which is narrow and reductionist. It is our view that in the implementation of the revised curriculum much, as ever, will depend on teachers and their professional judgement. The extent to which the post-Dearing curriculum is successful will depend on the skill and enthusiasm with which teachers can convert it into interesting and valuable experiences for children. This is no less true of humanities than of other subjects.

The new inspection framework for schools is having some interesting effects on school priorities. There is a clear obligation on inspection teams to ascertain the extent to which a school is meeting the requirements of Section 1 of the 1988 Act, namely to meet the cultural, moral and spiritual needs of the child. This overarching requirement subsumes detailed questions about particular subjects, levels of attainment and so on. But yet in the use of the terms cultural, moral and spiritual we see the recognition of key concerns within the humanities.

It is very encouraging to note that Nicholas Tate, the chief executive of SCAA, appointed in 1994, is clear about the centrality of questions of value in the National Curriculum.

> Defining the fundamental purposes of the curriculum is inseparable from defining our society and its values. Since Western societies have difficulty

with this, it is no wonder some schools have problems deciding what is meant by the moral, cultural and spiritual dimension of the curriculum. However, as the educational system leaves much of the responsibility for these matters to schools, it is in schools that the debate must take place.
(Tate, 1994)

We certainly hope that this book can contribute to that debate in schools and in the communities which they serve. To recognise the moral and cultural complexities of the curriculum and the schooling process is a long step beyond the crudeness of school league tables and such matters, which have dominated discussion for so long.

However, such a debate must also take place within teacher education (both pre-service and in-service). Here the difficulties of providing adequate preparation for intending teachers are only slightly ameliorated by the recent increase in centrally funded provision for humanities training for serving teachers, through 'GEST' courses. Initial teacher training has become such a political football during the early 1990s that it is difficult to predict its future with any certainty. The persistent attempts on initial courses to provide students with at least an introduction to all subjects in the primary curriculum have made some small impact. However, the difficulties of condensing a student's entire preparation for the teaching of history, geography or religious education into a course element of around 12 hours (a not untypical figure for each of these subjects on a 1-year PGCE route) are all too apparent. Many providers have developed imaginative ways of combining subjects and providing integrated experiences, often 'in the field', in order to make the most of limited time. Throughout this book we have included examples which draw on our own work with student teachers at the University of the West of England, within our Faculty, in schools and overseas.

One of the more positive features of recent years, however, has been the increased opportunity for undergraduate students to carry out school-based research relating to their specialist subject. So for example, geography and history students have undertaken significant, though small scale, pieces of action research and curriculum development working with teachers and children in primary classrooms. Again, we have made use of some of these studies in this book. This work has encouraged students to be confident in asking questions about *why* things are as they are. In other words they have been exploring questions about values and morality, rather than simply teaching effectiveness or other 'performance indicators'.

With respect to in-service work, there has been growing provision for subject co-ordinators, through the 'GEST' scheme. The provision of such courses is not only a response to the demands of National Curriculum *per se*. It is also a reflection of the continuing creeping tendency for children in the last 2 years of primary school to be taught for part of the time by subject specialists. This is an idea which has been promoted in a number of places, but particularly by Professor Alexander and HMI Rose (e.g. Alexander *et al.*, 1992). Chris Woodhead, in his role as Chief Inspector of Schools added to this pressure in his widely publicised annual report of 1995 (OFSTED, 1995). Research, such as that carried out by our colleague John Lee (1993) indicates that there is still little evidence of schools actually providing such specialist teaching, but it remains a popular idea in influential circles. The obstacles are mainly logistical and do seem to be considerable, especially in smaller primary schools. In this book we have demonstrated some of the richness which can be achieved through working across subject divisions and in deriving programmes of learning from topics.

This is not to deny the importance of teachers' subject knowledge (*see* Bennett and Carre, 1993). It may, however, be more effective to utilise teachers' subject knowledge through their co-ordination of a subject within a school, than to offer teaching by a specialist. The role of the subject co-ordinator includes drawing up curriculum plans and supporting colleagues as necessary in their work in the particular subject.

Stepping back now from the immediate world of schools, we can observe that the wider world in which children are growing up is a world of rapid change. Perhaps one of the most significant areas of change is that of information technology. The speed and efficiency with which it is possible for information to be communicated around this planet have been increasing exponentially. However, both the speed and the efficiency are dependent upon the availability of technology. This technology is not universally available, hence the issues of social justice and the distribution of resources continue to be extremely important. In Western countries most young people do experience elements of the information society, most notably as consumers of mass media outputs, received on television monitors in the home.

This information society rarely recognises national borders. Although we may think of the nation state as the key unit of political analysis, when we think of the child as consumer and cultural being, the framework of experience is very clearly not a national one, but an international one. At a cultural level the dominant influences appear to be the USA and, increasingly, Japan and other Southeast Asian countries. The European dimension of citizenship is perhaps most powerful at the political level, where increasingly rights of movement and responsibilities relating to representation are determined. In Britain however, as indicated in Chapter

7, there still remains considerable distrust of European political institutions.

As the local provider of education for young children the primary school is a community based unit. However, given the significance of these wider contexts, it is essential that the perspectives of the staff and children in every school are also regional and global. This does not imply an uncritical acceptance of things European or technologies North American or Japanese. Rather it is a call for schools to help their children to examine critically the technological forms and political institutions and structures which exist in this wider world, the better to use them and develop them in line with the values which they come to hold as citizens. Our suggestion is that humanities is the area of learning which has the key responsibility for supporting such developments.

The power of humans to act in and upon the world has been demonstrated in such powerful ways during the last 15 years of this millennium. The collapse of the Berlin Wall and the liberation of South Africa from the oppression of apartheid are just two examples of the scale of political change which can be brought about through human agency, changes which many of us doubted we would see in our lifetimes. Virtual reality and the power of the CD-ROM may make their users better placed to understand the world and may help lead to solutions to problems, but they do not displace the centrality of questions of value. Indeed, the applications of such technologies are developed with values deeply implicit within them.

Markets constitute one system for the production and consumption of goods and services. But markets are essentially competitive and hence create 'losers' as well as 'winners'. It must be part of the purpose of humanities teaching to help learners see these processes at work and develop the ability to criticise and influence them. As Mark Lawson (1994) recalls 'Margaret Thatcher once memorably put a monetarist gloss on the parable of the Good Samaritan by explaining that he was able to give help only because he had been able to become rich'. This perspective on the Good Samaritan, and indeed her view that 'there is no such thing as society', contrast starkly with the perspectives explored in this book. Indeed, the children in Eastcombe Primary School (*see* Chapter 1) offered a very different analysis of the story of the Good Samaritan.

A survey carried out in late 1994 by the Mori organisation for BBC Radio 1 suggests that young people maintain a high level of confidence in schools as exemplars of 'good moral standards'. Considering the ways in which teachers have been pilloried in some sections of the press over recent years, this is an interesting finding. Indeed schools surpassed doctors, parents, police and the church as upholders of morality in this survey of 1200 people aged between 15 and 35 (*The Guardian*, 1994b).

To become genuinely active and principled citizens, children need to be able to discuss moral questions and to learn actively. There is no evidence that an inactive didactic mode of teaching and learning leads towards the development of such citizens, who can take a full part in democratic processes. Thus throughout this book our answer to the question 'How do children best learn humanities?' has been to emphasise talk, social learning and an active, experiential approach.

The role of the humanities teacher in helping children to decentre from their own perspectives, to develop empathy with their fellow citizens and to become explicit about their moral judgements is a major responsibility. It is our hope that the ideas in this book will have helped readers to understand these onerous but essential tasks which will in turn lead them to help children understand what it is that is special about being human.

# Appendix: Memorandum on Teaching and Learning about Human Rights in Schools

*(Adopted by the Committee of Ministers on 14 May 1985 at the 385th meeting of Ministers' Deputies)*

## Recommendation No. R (85) 7

The Committee of Ministers, under the terms of Article 15.*b* of the Statute of the Council of Europe.

Considering that the aim of the Council of Europe is to achieve a greater unity between its members for the purpose of safeguarding and realising the ideals and principles which are their common heritage:

Reaffirming the human rights undertakings embodied in the United Nations' Universal Declaration of Human Rights, the Convention for the Protection of Human Rights and Fundamental Freedoms and the European Social Charter:

Having regard to the commitments to human rights education made by member states at international and European conferences in the last decade:

Recalling:
– its own Resolution (78) 41 on 'The teaching of human rights'
– its Declaration on 'Intolerance: a threat to democaracy' of 14 May 1981.
– its Recommendation No. R (83) 13 on 'The role of the secondary school in preparing young people for life';

Noting Recommendation 963 (1983) of the Consultative Assembly of the Council of Europe on 'Cultural and educational means of reducing violence':

Concious of the need to reaffirm democratic values in the face of:
– intolerance, acts of violence and terrorism;
– the re-emergence of the public expression of racist and xenophobic attitudes;
– the disillusionment of many young people in Europe, who are affected by the economic recession and aware of the continuing poverty and inequality in the world;

Believing, therefore, that, throughout their school career, all young people should learn about human rights as part of their preparation for life in a pluralistic democracy;

Convinced that schools are communities which can, and should, be an example of respect for the dignity of the individual and for difference, for tolerance, and for equality of opportunity,

I. Recommends that the governments of member states, having regard to their national education systems and to the legislative basis for them:

    *a.* encourage teaching and learning about human rights in schools in line with the suggestions contained in the appendix hereto;

    *b.* draw the attention of persons and bodies concerned with school education to the text of this recommendation;

II. Instructs the Secretary General to transmit this recommendation to the governments of those states party to the European Cultural Convention which are not members of the Council of Europe.

# Appendix to Recommendation No. R (85) 7: Suggestions for teaching and learning about human rights in schools

1.    *Human rights in the school curriculum*

1.1.    The understanding and experience of human rights is an important element of the preparation of all young people for life in a democratic and pluralistic society. It is part of social and political education, and it involves intercultural and international understanding.

1.2.    Concepts associated with human rights can, and should, be acquired from an early stage. For example, the non-violent resolution of a conflict and respect for other people can already be experienced within the life of a pre-school or primary class.

1.3.    Opportunities to introduce young people to more abstract notions of human rights, such as those involving an understanding of philosophical, political and legal concepts, will occur in the secondary school, in particular in such subjects as history, geography, social studies, moral and religious education, language and literature, current affairs and economics.

1.4.    Human rights inevitably involve the domain of politics. Teaching about human rights should, therefore, always have international agreements and covenants as a point of reference, and teachers should take care to avoid imposing their personal convictions on their pupils and involving them in ideological struggles.

2.    *Skills*

The skills associated with understanding and supporting human rights include:

    i.    *intellectual skills*, in particular:

– skills associated with written and oral expression, including the ability to listen and discuss, and to defend one's opinions:

– skills involving judgment, such as:

    – the collection and examination of material from various sources, including the mass media, and the ability to analyse it and to arrive at fair and balanced conclusions:

    – the identification of bias, prejudice, stereotypes and discrimination:

    ii.    *social skills*, in particular:

– recognising and accepting differences;

– establishing positive and non-oppressive personal relationships:

– resolving conflict in a non-violent way;

– taking responsibility;

– participating in decisions;

– understanding the use of the mechanisms for the protection of human rights at local, regional, European and world levels.

3. *Knowledge to be acquired in the study of human rights*

3.1. The study of human rights in schools will be approached in different ways according to age and circumstances of the pupil and the particular situations of schools and education systems. Topics to be covered in learning about human rights could include:

i. the main categories of human rights, duties, obligations and responsibilities;

ii. the various forms of injustice, inequality and discrimination, including sexism and racism;

iii. people, movements and key events, both successes and failures, in the historical and continuing struggle for human rights;

iv. the main international declarations and conventions on human rights, such as the Universal Declaration of Human Rights and the Convention for the Protection of Human Rights and Fundamental Fredoms.

3.2. The emphasis in teaching and learning about human rights should be positive. Pupils may be led to feelings of powerlessness and discouragement when confronted with many examples of violation and negations of human rights. Instances of progress and success should be used.

3.3. The study of human rights in schools should lead to an understanding of, and sympathy for, the concepts of justice, equality, freedom, peace, dignity, rights and democracy. Such understanding should be both cognitive and based on experience and feelings. Schools should, thus, provide opportunities for pupils to experience affective involvement in human rights and to express their feelings through drama, art, music, creative writing and audiovisual media.

4. *The climate of the school*

4.1. Democracy is best learned in a democratic setting where participation is encouraged, where views can be expressed openly and discussed, where there is freedom of expression for pupils and teachers, and where there is fairness and justice. An appropriate climate is, therefore, an essential complement to effective learning about human rights.

4.2. Schools should encourage participation in their activities by parents and other members of the community. It may well be appropriate for schools to work with non-governmental organisations which can provide information, case-studies and first-hand experience of successful campaigns for human rights and dignity.

4.3. Schools and teachers should attempt to be positive towards all their pupils, and recognize that all their achievements are important – whether they be academic, artistic, musical, sporting or practical.

5. *Teacher training*

5.1. The initial training of teachers should prepare them for their future contribution to teaching about human rights in their schools. For example, future teachers should:

i. be encouraged to take an interest in national and world affairs;

ii. have the chance of studying or working in a foreign country or a different enviroment;

iii. be taught to identify and combat all forms of discrimination in schools and society and be encouraged to confront and overcome their own prejudices.

5.2    Future and practising teachers should be encouraged to familiarise themselves with:

i.    the main international declarations and conventions on human rights;

ii.    the working and achievements of the international organisations which deal with the protection and promotion of human rights, for example through visits and study tours.

5.3    All teachers need, and should be given the opportunity, to update their knowledge and to learn new methods through in-service training. This could include the study of good practice in teaching about human rights, as well as the development of appropriate methods and materials.

5.    *International Human Rights Day*

Schools and teacher training establishments should be encouraged to observe International Human Rights Day (10 December).

# References

Alexander, R., Rose, J. and Woodhead, C. (1992) *Curriculum Organisation and Practice*. London: DES.

Antonouris, G. and Wilson, J. (1989) *Equal Opportunities in Schools: New Dimensions in Topic Work*. London: Cassell.

Anand, I. (1988) *King Jahangir and the Baby*. London: Andre Deutsch.

Austen, J. (1965) *Persuasion*. London: Oxford University Press.

Avon County Council (1993a) Children developing as readers. *The Avon Collaborative Reading Project – An Analysis and Evaluation*. Bristol: Avon County Council.

Avon County Council (1993b) *Mystery and Meaning: The Agreed Syllabus for Religious Education in Avon*. Bristol: Avon County Council.

Bale, J. (1987) *Geography in the Primary School*. London: Routledge and Kegan Paul.

Bantock, G. (1969) 'Discovery Methods', in Cox, C. and Dyson, A. (eds) *Black Paper Two*, Critical Quarterly Society.

Barber, M. (1994) *The Making of the 1944 Education Act*. London: Cassell.

Barnes, D. (1976) *From Communication to Curriculum*. Harmondsworth: Penguin.

Bell, G.H. (1991) *Developing a European Dimension in Primary Schools*. London: David Fulton.

Bennett, N. and Carré, C. (eds)(1993) *Learning to Teach*. London: Routledge and Kegan Paul.

Bennett, S.N. and Dunne, E. (1992) *Managing Classroom Groups*. Hemel Hempstead: Simon Schuster Education.

Bennett, S.N., Desforges, C., Cockburn, A. and Wilkinson, B. (1984) *The Quality of Pupil Learning Experience*. London: Lawrence Erlbaum Associates.

BFSS National RE Centre (1988) *Tell Me a Story – Story and Religious Education*. London: WLIHE and London Borough of Hounslow.

Biott, C. and Easden, P. (eds)(1994) *Collaborative Learning in Staffrooms and Classrooms*. London: David Fulton.

Birley, R. (1955) *The Undergrowth of History. Some Traditional Stories of English History Reconsidered*. London: Historical Association.

Blyth, W.A.L. (1990) *Making the Grade for Primary Humanities – Assessment in the Humanities*. Milton Keynes: Open University Press.

Blyth, J. and Low-Beer, A. (1991) *Teaching History to Younger Children*. London: Historical Association.

Boardman, D. (1983) *Graphicacy and Geography Teaching*. London: Croom Helm.

Bristol Broadsides (1983) *St Pauls People Talking to Children from St Barnabas School*. Bristol: Bristol Broadsides.

Bruner, J.S. (1960) *The Process of Instruction*. Cambridge, Ma.: Harvard University Press.

Campbell, J. and Little, V. (1989) *Humanities in the Primary School*. Lewes: Falmer Press.

Carr, E.H. (1964) *What is History?* Harmondsworth: Penguin.

Carson, R. (1963) *Silent Spring*. Harmondsworth: Penguin.

Cashmore, E. (1987) *The Logic of Racism*. London: Allen & Unwin

Centre for Educational Research and Innovation (1991) *Environment, Schools and Active Learning*. Paris: OECD

Clendinnen, I. (1991) *Aztecs*. Cambridge: CUP

Clough, N. and Menter, I. (1993) 'Developing education for environmental citizenship in the new Europe: some lessons from cross-cultural experience', paper presented at 'Culture, Ecology, Pedagogical Process' Conference, held at Daugavpils, Latvia, October.

Cole, M., Clay, J. and Hill, D. (1990/91) 'The citizen as individual and nationalist or social and internationalist? What is the role of education?', *Critical Social Policy*, **30**, 68–87.

Collicott, S.L. (1992) 'Who is forgotten in HSU, 'Britain Since the 1930s'?', *Primary Teaching Studies*, **6**, (3), 252–268.

Collicott, S.L. (1993) 'A way of looking at history: local–national–world links', *Teaching History*, **July,** 18–23.

Colton, R.W. and Morgan, R.F. (1974) *Schools Council Project Environment*. London: Longman.

Cooper, H. (1992) *The Teaching of History – Implementing the National Curriculum*. London: David Fulton.

Copley, T. and Priestly, J. (1991) *Forms of Assessment in Religious Education – The main report of the FARE project*. Exeter: FARE.


Daniels, A. and Sinclair, S. (1985) *People before Places*. Birmingham: Development Education Centre.

Dearden, R.F. (1976) *Problems in Primary Education*. London: Routledge and Kegan Paul.

DES (1967) *Children and their Primary Schools (The Plowden Report)*. London: HMSO.

DES (1978) *Primary Education in England. A survey by H.M. Inspectors for Schools*. London: HMSO.

DES (1985) *Education for All (The Swann Report)*. London: HMSO.

DES (1989a) *Teaching and Learning of History and Geography*. London HMSO.

DES (1989b) *Environmental Education from 5 to 16: Curriculum Matters 13*. London: HMSO.

DES (1989c) *Personal and Social Education from 5 to 16: Curriculum Matters 14*. London: HMSO.

DES (1989d) *The Education Reform Act 1988: Religious Education and Collective Worship, Circular 3/89*. London: DES.

DES (1990) *National Curriculum: History Working Group Final Report*. London: HMSO.

DFE (1994) *Religious Education and Collective Worship, Circular 1/94*. London: DFE.

DFE (1995a) *History in the National Curriculum*. London: HMSO.

DFE (1995b) *Geography in the National Curriculum*. London: HMSO.

Donaldson, M. (1978) *Children's Minds*. London: Fontana.

Drummond, M.J. (1993) *Assessing Children's Learning*. London: David Fulton.

Du Garde Peach, L. (1961) *Stone Age Man in Britain. An Adventure from History*. Loughborough: Wills and Hepworth.

Eke, R. (1986) 'Media Education Issues' in *Working Papers Two*, BFI/DES. National Working Party on Primary Media Education. London: BFI.

Fines, J. and Verrier, R. (1974) *The Drama of History: An Experiment in Co-operative Teaching*. London: New University Education.

Fisher, S. and Hicks, D. (1985) *World Studies 8–13: A Teachers Handbook*. London: Oliver and Boyd.

Flanagan, L. (1992) 'Reconstructing a Primary History Curriculum for Equality', unpublished BEd dissertation. Bristol: University of the West of England.

Flanders, N. (1970) *Analysing Teacher Behaviour*. Reading, Ma.: Addison–Wesley.

Galton, M. (1995) *Crisis in the Primary Classroom*. London: David Fulton.

Galton, M., Simon, B. and Croll, P. (1980) *Inside the Primary Classroom*. London: Routledge and Kegan Paul.

Garner, R. (1994) 'Out goes 1066 and all that', *Daily Mirror*, **5 May**.

Geographical Association (1992) *Primary Geography Matters; Changes in the Primary Curriculum*. Sheffield: Geographical Association.

Goalen, P. and Hendy, L. (1994) 'Its not just fun, it works!' Developing children's historical thinking through drama. *The Curriculum Journal*, **4 (3)**, 363–84.

Graham, D. (1993) *A Lesson for Us All – The Making of the National Curriculum*. London: Routledge.

Graham, D. and Lynn, X. (1989) 'Mud huts and flints – children's images of the Third World', *Education 3-13*, **17**, 2.

Grieve, R. and Hughes, M. (1990) *Understanding Children*. Oxford: Basil Blackwell.

*Guardian* (1994a) 'Thou shalt have a new moral code', **10 October**.

*Guardian* (1994b) 'Poorest 10 per cent no better off than in 1967', **3 June**.

Hadow Committee (1931) *Report of the Committee on the Primary School*. London: HMSO.

Haggett, P. (3rd edn)(1983) *Geography: A Modern Synthesis*. London: Harper & Row.

Hallam, R.R. (1979) 'Attempting to improve logical thinking in school history', *Research in Education*, **21**, 1–24.

Hammond, J. and Hay, D. (1990) *New Methods in RE teaching; An Experiential Approach*. London: Oliver & Boyd.

Hansard, House of Lords, (1988) Vol 493 Col 1453 – 1486, 26 February.

Hardy, J. and Vieler-Porter, C. (1990) 'Race, schooling and the 1988 Education Reform Act' in Flude, M. and Hammer, M. (eds) *The Education Reform Act 1988*. London: Falmer Press.

Harnett, P. (1991) 'Reading pictures', in *Primary Historian*, pp.4–6.

Harnett, P. (1993) 'Identifying progression in children's understanding: the use of visual materials to assess primary school children's learning in history', *Cambridge Journal of Education*, **23(2)**, 137–54.

Hicks, D. (ed.) (1988) *Education for Peace*. London: Routledge.

Hicks, D. (1994) *Educating for the Future: A Practical Classroom Guide*. London: World Wide Fund for Nature.

Hicks, D. and Steiner, M. (1989) *Making Global Connections*. Edinburgh: Oliver and Boyd.

Hohmann, M., Bernard, B. and Weikart, D. (1979) *Young Children in Action – a manual for pre-school educators*. Ypsilanti, Michicen: High Scope Press.

Hillgate Group (1986) *Whose Schools? A Radical Manifesto*. London: Hillgate Group.

HMI (1985) *History in the Primary and Secondary Years*. London: HMSO.

HMI (1989) *Aspects of Primary Education: The Teaching and Learning of History and Geography*. London: HMSO.

HMI (1994) *Primary Matters*. London: HMSO.

Holm, J. (1976) *Teaching Religion*. Oxford: Oxford University Press.

Holt J. (1965) *How Children Fail*. London: Penguin.

Howells, G. (1994) 'The use of computers within the history curriculum', unpublished BEd dissertation. Bristol: University of the West of England.

Huckle, J. (1988) 'Environment', in Hicks, D. (ed.) *Education for Peace*. London: Routledge.

Hughes, S. (1978) *Dogger*. London: Bodley Head.

Hull, J. (1993) *The Place of Christianity in the Curriculum: The Theology of the Department for Education (Hockerill Lecture)*. Hockerill Educational Foundation.

Kearney, H. (1994) 'Four nations or one?' in Bourdillon, H. (ed.) *Teaching History*. London: Routledge.

Keegan, J. (1994) 'History meets its Waterloo when lunacy is in command', *Daily Telegraph*, **5 May**.

King, A. and Reiss, M. (eds) (1993) *The Multicultural Dimension of the National Curriculum*. London: Falmer Press.

Knight, P. (1992) 'Myth and legend at Key Stage 1 – the case of Robin Hood', *Primary Teaching Studies*, **6(3)**, 237–44.

Knight, P. (1993) *Primary Geography, Primary History*. London: David Fulton.

Lacey, C. and Williams, R. (eds) (1987) *Education, Ecology and Development (The Case for an Education Network)*. London: WWF and Kogan Page.

Lamont, G. and Burns, S. (1993) *Values and Visions: spiritual development and global awareness in the primary school*. Manchester: Manchester Development Education Project.

Lee, J. (1993) 'Curriculum in Key Stage 2'. Paper presented at British Educational Research Association Conference, September, Liverpool.

Lee, L. (1959) *Cider with Rosie*. London: Hogarth Press.

Lynch, J. (1992) *Education for Citizenship in a Multicultural Society*. London: Cassell.

Lynn, S. (1993) 'Children Reading Pictures: History Visuals at Key Stages 1 and 2'. *Education 3-13*, **21(3)**, 23–29.

McGovern, C. (1994) *The SCAA Review of National Curriculum History: A Minority Report*. York: Campaign for Real Education.

Martin, G. and Turner, E. (eds) (1972) *Environmental Studies*. London: Blond Educational Leicester.

Mays, P. (1985) *Teaching Children Through the Environment*. London: Hodder and Stoughton.

Milne, S. (1994) 'Communitarianism: Blah, blah, Blair…', *The Guardian*, **7 October**.

Milner, D. (1985) *Children and Race Ten Years On*. London: Ward Lock.

Mlewa, S. (1994) 'Towards understanding religious education in the primary school', unpublished assignment for DfE Curriculum Co-ordinators Course. Bristol: University of the West of England.

National Curriculum Council (1990a) *The Whole Curriculum (Curriculum Guidance 3)*. York: NCC.

National Curriculum Council (1990b) *Environmental Education (Curriculum Guidance 7)*. York: NCC.

National Curriculum Council (1990c ) *Education for Citizenship (Curriculum Guidance 8)*. York: NCC.

National Curriculum Council (1993a) *Spiritual and moral development – a discussion paper*. York: NCC.

National Curriculum Council (1993b) *Religious education in the basic curriculum in England and Wales*. York: NCC.

Norman, K. (1990) *Teaching, Talking and Learning in Key Stage 1, A Booklet for Teachers Based on the National Oracy Project*. York: National Curriculum Council.

O'Hare, C. B. (1987) 'The effect of verbal labelling in books of visual perception: an experimental investigation', *Educational Research*, **29**, 3.

O'Riordan, T. (1989) 'The challenge for environmentalism', in Peet, R. and Thrift, N. (eds) *New Models in Geography Vol 1: The Political Economy Perspective*. London: Unwin Hyman.

OECD (1993) *Environmental Education: An Approach to Sustainable Development*. Paris: OECD.

OFSTED (1994) *Religious Education and Collective Worship; 1992–1993*. London: HMSO.

Pankhania, J. (1994) *Liberating the National History Curriculum*. Lewes: Falmer Press.

Perry, G.A., Jones, E. and Hammersley, A. (1968)(revised edn., 1971) *Teachers' Handbook for Environmental Studies*. London: Blandford Press.

Pike, G. and Selby, D. (1988) *Global Teacher, Global Learner*. London: Hodder and Stoughton.

Pollard, A. and Tann, S. (1993) (2nd edn.) *Reflective Teaching in the Primary School*. London: Cassell.

Pollard, A., Broadfoot, P., Croll, P., Osborn, M. and Abbott, D. (1994) *Changing English Primary Education?* London: Cassell.

PRINDEP (1990) 'Teachers and children in PNP classroom'. *Evaluation Report 11*. University of Leeds Primary Needs Independent Evaluation Project.

Proctor, (1985) 'Redefining the basis of primary education', *Education 3–13*, **3(1)**, 5–8.

Read, G., *et al.*, (1992) *How do I Teach R.E.? Westhill Project 5–16*. Cheltenham: Stanley Thornes.

Rowe, D. and Newton, J. (eds) (1994) *You, Me, Us: Social and Moral Responsibility for Primary Schools*. London: Citizenship Foundation.

Roycroft-Davis, C. (1994) 'Britain's glorious past banished from lessons', *The Sun*, **5 May**.

Sandbach, F. (1980) *Environment, Ideology and Policy*. Oxford: Blackwell.

SARI (1994) *Report for SARI*. Bristol: SARI.

SCAA (1994a) *History in the National Curriculum: Draft Proposals*. London: DFE.

SCAA (1994b) *The National Curriculum and its Assessment*. London: SCAA.

SCAA (1994c) *Religious Education: Model Syllabuses for Religious Education*. London: SCAA.

SCAA (1994d) *The National Curriculum Orders*. London: SCAA.

Schools Council History 13–16 Project (1976) *A New Look at History.* Edinburgh: Holmes McDougall.

Shrimsley, R. (1994) 'British history best, says Patten', *The Daily Telegraph*, **19 March**.

Starkey, H. (ed.) (1991) *The Challenge of Human Rights Education.* London: Council of Europe with Cassell

Starkey, H. (1992) 'Education for Citizenship in France' in Jones, E. and Jones, N. (eds) *Education for Citizenship.* London: Kogan Page.

Steiner, M. (1994) *Learning from Experience.* Stoke-on-Trent: Trentham Books.

Strong, R. and Oman, J.T. (1971) *Elizabeth R.* London: Secker and Warburgh.

Tate, N. (1994) 'Target vision', *Times Educational Supplement*, **2 December**, 19.

Terry, F. (1989) 'Women's History and Children's Perceptions of Gender', *Teaching History*, **20 July**, 2.

Thatcher, M. (1993) *The Downing Street Years.* London: Harper/Collins.

Thornton, S.J. and Vukelich, R. (1988) 'Effects of children's understanding of time concepts on historical understanding', *Theory and Research in Social Education*, **xvi, i**, 69–82.

Tizard, B., Blatchford. P., Burke, J., Farquhar, C. and Plewis, I. (1988) *Young Children at School in the Inner City.* London: Erlbaum.

Tulasiewicz, W. (1993) 'The European dimension and the national curriculum', in King, A.S. and Reiss, M.J. (eds) *The Multicultural Dimension and the National Curriculum.* Lewes: Falmer Press.

Vidal, J. (1994) 'DIY politics', *The Guardian*, **7 October**.

Vygotsky, L. S. (1962) *Thought and Language.* Cambridge: MIT Press.

Vygotsky, L.S. (1978) *Mind in Society: the Development of Higher Psychological Processes*, Cambridge, Ma.: Harvard University Press.

Wadell, M. and Dupasquier, P. (1983) *Going West.* London: Anderson Press.

Walford, R. (ed.) (1985) *Geographical Education for a Multicultural Society.* Sheffield: Geographical Association.

Walford, R. (ed.) (1991) *Viewpoint on Geography Teaching.* Harlow: Longmans.

Ward, C. and Fyson, A. (1973) *Streetwork: The Exploding School.* London: Routledge and Kegan Paul.

Watson, B. (1993) *The effective teaching of religious education.* London: Longmans.

West, J. (1986) 'The development of primary school children's sense of the past', in Fairbrother, R. (ed.) Greater Manchester Primary Contact, *History and the Primary School*, Special Issue 6. Manchester: Didsbury School of Education.

Wiegand, P. (1992) *Places in the Primary School.* Lewes: Falmer Press.

Wiegand, P. (1993) *Children and Primary Geography.* London: Cassell.

Whittell, G. (1988) *The Story of the Three Whales.* Walker Books.

Williams, R. (1989) *One Earth Many Worlds*, United Kingdom: WWF.

Wiltshire County Council (1987) *Using Stories in Religious Education.* Swindon: Wiltshire County Council.

Wood, A. and Richardson, R. (1992) *Inside Stories: Wisdom and Hope for Changing Worlds.* Stoke-on-Trent: Trentham.

Wood, T. (1982) *Playback: History Roleplays.* London: Edward Arnold.

Wray, D. and Lewis, M. (1994) 'Information Desk', *Junior Education*, **18**, 30–31.

Zidovske Muzeum (1993) *I have not seen a butterfly around here: children's drawings and poems from Terezin.* Prague: Zidovske Muzeum.

# Index

198